"My brother Manny Ohonme's life and mission is living proof that miracles still exist! A young shoeless Nigerian boy has become a strong leader who is impacting the world by spreading the love of Jesus Christ through the very thing he once lacked: shoes! Manny, you have inspired me to take the hill!"

— **Damien Horne**, *International recording artist (MuzikMafia)*

"Manny, thank you for being willing to step out on faith, accept the calling, make the enormous financial, family, and time sacrifices necessary to drive this ministry. You have truly been a blessing to me, my company, and my family."

— **Paul Thompson**, *CEO, Transportation Insight*

"From a shoeless 9-year-old boy who was shown love and compassion by a missionary by giving him his first pair of shoes and introducing him to the Lord of his life, Manny has become an ambassador to the world showing that same act of kindness. He brings faith and hope to the hopeless, compassion to the poor, love to a world filled with hurt and pain, and joy to those in need. It is with a servant's heart that he ministers to his neighbors all over the world as he brings honor and glory to the name of Jesus."

— **Cathy Hendrick**, *Hendrick Motorsports*

"Over the past two years, I've enjoyed learning about and actually participating in the work of Samaritan's Feet. It has been a privilege of partnering with Manny and his work, specifically in Burundi, seeing thousands of lives touched by new shoes and the sharing of the Gospel of Jesus Christ to the poorest of the poor. Manny's deep heart of faith and compassion for the poor is the right example for many in the church today. It's a privilege to call Manny and Samaritan's Feet my friend and colleague in the Gospel of grace."

— **David Chadwick**, *senior pastor, Forest Hill Church in Charlotte, NC*

"A dad should be someone who can follow God, lead his family and work hard doing what he loves. In all three of these areas my dad does an amazing job."
— **Nike Ohonme**, *oldest daughter and future CEO, Samaritan's Feet*

"My dad doesn't just provide hope for others, but also mostly me. I always know whatever I do he is behind me even if it wasn't his choice. If I need help he is there even when I don't want him to be."
— **Dele Ohonme**, *second daughter, future editor-in-chief and world changer*

"My dad is inspiring to us all. He is fun, he is also the founder of a ministry, he is a great dad. I love him and he is probably the nicest person I have ever met. He is a hard worker. Thanks for being my dad."
— **Yemi Ohonme**, *youngest daughter, world changer and future doctor*

"I love my Dad. He is the greatest Dad in the world."
— **Wale Ohonme**, *youngest son, future president, Samaritan's Feet*

SOLE PURPOSE

SHOES OF HOPE FROM THE FEET OF A SAMARITAN

EMMANUEL "MANNY" OHONME
WITH KYLE WHELLISTON

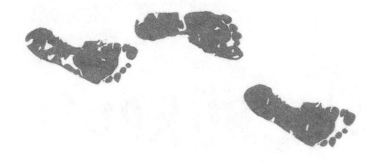

Sole Purpose

ISBN: 978-0-9824145-9-0

Published by

LifeBridge

Books
P.O. Box 49428
Charlotte, NC 28277

Interior book design by Roni Lagin. Cover design by JR Graphics.
Photographs courtesy of the author. Used by permission.
Printed in the United States of America.

DEDICATION

This book is dedicated to Tracie Lynn Ohonme, my beloved wife of noble character who has believed and seen the God potential in me since we met on that cold winter evening in Devils Lake, North Dakota, in 1990. Her faith, resolve, and confidence in me have taught me that with God no mountain is too high to climb and reminds me that I can do all things through Him who gives me strength. She has opened her arms to the poor, and extended her hands to the needy. Many women in history have done noble things, but my bride Tracie surpasses them all.

Thank you for loving me the way you do, my life was made complete the day I met you. I love you "forever and a day" – FAAD!

To my first ministry, my four bundles of joy that the Lord entrusted to my care, without whom life has little meaning. My daughters—to Adenike ("Nike"), in the Yoruba language of Nigeria meaning "our princess' crown is worth being preserved"; to Oladele ("Dele") meaning "success has come home"; to Oluyemisi ("Yemi") meaning "God Provided You to Bless Me"; and to my son Adewale ("Wale") meaning "royalty has come home."

To my mom Florence Ibiyemi Ohonme who taught me to dream and believe that the impossible can become possible when you believe. You've shown me that the reason God created the sky so high was so poor boys like me could dream real big.

Thank you, mom, for planting the seed of faith early in my life and teaching me to say "Yes" to the Lord. Your life has taught me that God's delay is never His denial.

To my father David Bamidele Ohonme, whom I look forward to celebrate eternity with in heaven someday together with my Lord.

To all my brothers and sisters and extended family around the world.

To every missionary, volunteer, and servant of the Lord who sacrifices daily and leaves the comfort of life and their homes, so children like me in all nations can hear the good news and the message of hope. Know that your labor is not in vain. I am living proof and the seed of your labor of love.

To Dave from Wisconsin, thank you for the gift of a pair of shoes; whoever knew that a pair of shoes could change the world?

To the millions of orphans and vulnerable children in Africa and around the globe—Dream BIG, and know that the impossible is available for you! "He knows your name, rise up and let your light shine."

CONTENTS

FOREWORDS: A CHORUS OF VOICES

DR. SKI CHILTON – PROFESSOR, WAKE FOREST UNIVERSITY SCHOOL OF MEDICINE

In one monumental moment, God utilized my dear friend Manny Ohonme and an orphan in a South African shanty town known as Masoyi to completely "mess me up" for a lifetime, for an eternity.

Two years ago, my wife Briana and I had the opportunity to go with Manny to the shanty town of Masoyi, South Africa, to work with orphans affected by HIV/AIDS. Before leaving, I had not given the trip much thought. While I am a Christian and have a deep faith in God, I honestly had not prepared myself for what was to be my great moment with destiny.

I travel a great deal, but had never been to Africa. I thought at a minimum, I would be able to check off this continent from my not-visited list!

Upon arrival in Johannesburg, we were met at the gate by this very large African man named Manny who had a smile that seemed to saturate the entire airport. And everywhere this man moved, he was accompanied by children and laughter. Our 30-hour trip was followed by a six-hour school bus ride to our location. Following a few hours of sleep, we were up the next morning with breakfast and a devotion from this big man with the big smile. At the devotion, he promised us that we were about to be "messed up."

I remember looking at him as if he were crazy. I thought, "You don't know me. I am a world class scientist, a former professor at Johns Hopkins University School of Medicine, and the publisher of three books. I have seen everything."

Each day we gathered hundreds of shoes and began to wash the feet of the orphans. We gave them shoes, and prayed with them. My job was to pray with the orphans after they received their shoes. I would ask them how I could pray for them, and I received answers from these ten-to-twelve year old heads of households. I was not prepared for this, and it absolutely broke my heart. My group directly interacted with almost 2,000 orphans during our Masoyi stay.

On the third day of our trip, we traveled to a banana plantation. It was the saddest place I'd ever been, and I immediately knew my life would forever be changed. At 50 years old, I knew I was about to be "messed up," and there was absolutely nothing I could do about it.

When we arrived, hundreds of children were playing in a big field surrounded by a fence. The older ones stuck their heads through the fence, like trapped livestock, to get a better look at us. About 50 infants, all under two years old, were sitting in the mud crying. When I asked a caretaker the name of one infant, she couldn't answer. The baby was one of hundreds of children without names, looked after by a few "grannies."

I was immediately drawn to one of the infants. His eyes were deep yellow from liver failure as a result of AIDS and tuberculosis, his face badly distorted from a birth defect and the ravages of malnutrition. He was crying, too, but only halfheartedly. As I looked at him, I thought, "I can't pick him up; it's too much of a risk for me and my family." As a biomedical researcher, I knew the ramifications of contracting a drug resistant strain of tuberculosis.

Then, with great clarity, I heard for the first time in my life God's voice asking me: "Who are you?" And then, "*Whose* are you?"

I immediately picked up the child, washed his face, and sang the lullaby that my mom had sung to me when I was a baby.

The infant stopped crying and looked me right in the eyes. And in his eyes, I saw the face of God for the very first time in my life. And then I heard the echo of words from Mother Teresa: "We consider it an honor and privilege to serve Christ in the distressing disguise of the poorest of the poor with our humble work."

And that was the moment my dear African brother Manny had

predicted. I was now "messed up" and from that moment on, a majority of my life's work in one way or another has been focused on the plight of orphans and vulnerable children.

More recently, I went to an area called Jach, located on the border between southern Sudan and Darfur. On the second day of my trip there, when it was discovered that I was a researcher in the area of nutrition, I was brought an orphan child who was four years old but was so severely malnourished that she weighed twelve pounds. Her name was Abuk. She had been orphaned as a result of the surrounding genocide, and she was obviously just days from death. Over the next 10 days, I was blessed to be able to love that child, and to help bring her back to life by providing basic nutrition.

There are more than 140 million orphans worldwide, and 16 million in southern Africa who have lost their parents to AIDS. That number is expected to exceed 25 million in the next two years; that's two and a half times the population of North Carolina, my home state. Millions more have been orphaned as a result of genocide. When we talk about malnutrition, we are talking about millions of beautiful, loving children like Abuk. And I know that we must do something now to help children like her.

These young lives are malnourished by the amount and the type of food they eat. When it doesn't kill, malnutrition:

- Is responsible for hundreds of thousands of serious birth defects each year.
- Impairs mental development and stunts physical growth.
- Weakens immune function and renders children susceptible to infectious diseases, including malaria, tuberculosis, and HIV.
- Diminishes their capacity to work when they grow up, which undermines an entire nation's prospects for economic stability.

The orphans of Africa—in particular, the Masoyi orphans of South Africa and the Darfur orphans of Sudan—have deeply inspired me with their extraordinary hope, courage, and love, and, in the process, they have fundamentally and eternally transformed me.

I have decided to stand shoulder to shoulder with my dear friend Manny to devote the rest of my life to using the latest, most sophisticated first-world technology to help alleviate the suffering of African children. I have founded a nonprofit organization called Gene Smart Compassion that works with Manny and Samaritan's Feet to build homes, set up feeding stations, and to develop a therapeutic food designed to provide malnourished orphans with the micro-and macro-nutrients that they will need to survive and prosper given their current food supply.

I am compelled to say the same thing Manny would say: *we must do something now.* We individually and as a society will be judged by how we respond to the children. Millions of them are missing their "window of opportunity" for normal growth and development; thousands are dying every day. As the late Nobel laureate Gabriela Mistral wrote: "We are guilty of many errors and many faults, but our worst crime is abandoning the children, neglecting the foundation of life. Many of the things we need can wait. The child cannot. Right now is the time his bones are being formed, his blood is being made and his senses are being developed. To him we cannot answer 'Tomorrow.' His name is 'Today.'"

ERNIE JOHNSON – HOST, "NBA ON TNT," TURNER BROADCASTING

My career as a sportscaster has afforded me the opportunity to witness unforgettable moments, and to deal with some of the sports world's greatest performers on a one-on-one basis. At the same time, there are superstars to be found outside the boundaries of a playing field or a court. Manny Ohonme is such a man.

I first learned of Manny's mission one night when my wife Cheryl and I were watching the evening news and saw that ABC's "Person of the Week" was a college basketball coach named Ron Hunter, who coached a game in his bare feet. The story detailed "Samaritan's Feet" and the work of this guy, Manny, who wanted to put 10 million pairs of shoes on 10 million kids' feet, worldwide. Having a coach go barefoot was just one way of getting the word out about the organization.

Little did I know that several weeks later, while speaking at a Final Four event, I would have the chance to meet Manny. With that, my involvement with Samaritan's Feet began. Hearing his tales of worldwide travel, of kids receiving shoes for the first time, and of lives being changed by a message of God's love, were inspiring beyond measure. Being part of a shoe distribution has impacted me deeply. We wash feet, hand out new socks and shoes, speak to people who have been in many cases forgotten by society, and join hands in prayer.

11

My goal in life is to model the life of Jesus Christ. He is the Son of Man who came to serve, and not be served. Knowing this challenges me.

God has blessed me with a loving family, and a career in sports that allows me to basically talk about fun and games, and at times insulate me from "the real world." He has also blessed me with a chance meeting with Manny Ohonme which has opened my eyes to "the real world," where the gift of new shoes, or unexpected conversation, or a moment of prayer can not only brighten a day, but be the spark for a changed life.

I know that Manny's mission and his modeling of Jesus Christ has changed mine and challenged me more than I can ever express.

IBRAHIM ADULKAREEM SANI ABACHA — YOUTH WITH A MISSION (YWAM)

I was born and raised in a traditional Muslim family in Nigeria who missed no step in preparing me for life-long adherence to Islam. When Jesus found me, I gave my whole life to Him and completely revoked Islam. I was rejected by my own family, who even persecuted me to the edge of death. With the help of compassionate Christian leaders, I was able to find my way to a whole different part of Nigeria to a ministry called Gidan Bege, meaning "House of Hope."

I'm a firm believer in hope today because of a fifteen minute conversation I had in Nigeria in 2005 with a stranger from America who had come to bring me a pair of shoes. That conversation was monumental and helped birth my unyielding drive to see beyond the pain of this generation; I search for a new person inside every broken and wounded heart. I choose to see good in our broken and hopeless generation today because the man I met in Nigeria refused to let me go even though people lost hope in me, including my own family. This stranger gave me a hope to hold on to.

Emmanuel ("Manny") Ohonme said to me, "There's a man in you with a story that a generation deserves to hear and receive healing from. I will do whatever I can to support and uplift you so that you embrace all that God has called you to live for. Please do not give up on yourself; you have a story for the world! Every nation deserves to hope again and your story can and will inspire them to do so."

"What do you want to do with your life?" Manny asked. I told him that I wanted all that God has called me to do, especially working with Youth With A Mission (YWAM), starting in Jeffrey's Bay, South Africa. Manny and his wife, Tracie, gave me all the money for my flight to South Africa to begin my journey in missions with YWAM. Manny, his family, and his organization became my supporters and, most importantly, my family. He has left an indelible mark on my life since that moment in 2005.

The hope he whispered that day does not stop echoing in my heart every moment, especially when everything else seems hopeless. I became a motivational speaker for Christ so that through Him I can give those I speak to a reason to live for something beyond their sores. I speak with faith, hope, and all the courage I have left in my soul because I want this generation to know that they matter. All of this is a result of that moment with Manny Ohonme; he is now my mentor because I trust him with all my heart.

He made me believe that where you live should no longer determine whether you live.

SUE SEMRAU – HEAD COACH, FLORIDA STATE WOMEN'S BASKETBALL

The expressions on their faces pierced me.

And not in a superficial way. Not in a way that I would easily forget. These were smiles, pure and joyful smiles, from hearts that have hurt too much in their short lives.

That's what makes Samaritan's Feet so significant—so special. It meets basic, but vital, needs in a complicated world.

I knew the moment I sat in my office during the spring of 2009 and stumbled upon an article about IUPUI coach Ron Hunter coaching barefoot to raise awareness for Samaritan's Feet that this was something I wanted to be involved in. After I read Manny's story and testimony, I knew I could help. I never would have guessed the impact it would have on me or the Florida State women's basketball family in such a short time since.

It started when I went barefoot on the bench at the Donald L. Tucker Center, our home court, during an upset win over the then-No. 8 North

Carolina Tar Heels. While that produced headlines and write-ups about the cause, it wasn't enough. How often in our lives do we stop there? How often do we take an easy, comfortable step towards helping someone, but we never actually follow through and do it?

That's the thing about Samaritan's Feet, and more specifically our Lord: we are called to action. We are called to serve our world. We are called to help the helpless. It is so easy to talk about helping, but we can always find some sort of excuse not to follow through.

I didn't want that to be the case for me. Samaritan's Feet is too important a cause not to follow through.

I had the honor of joining a group of 15 people on a trip across the Atlantic to Nigeria during the summer of 2009. It was one of the most challenging experiences of my life. Poverty can be pushed to a far corner of our mind while we are consumed in our daily routines, but when you see it face-to-face it becomes such a reality. It can shake you. You want to help everyone of them, but the question of "How?" lingers. It weighs on you. When I stepped back on the plane to head home, I knew I wasn't done with Samaritan's Feet.

Although it was extremely powerful, I sensed that I needed to do more. I think the temptation is there to allow ourselves to limit the idea of service to overseas trips and third world countries. It was so important for me to take the mission of Samaritan's Feet and make it relevant in my own community.

After discussions with my home church, Calvary Chapel Tallahassee, we decided to plan a shoe distribution for Tallahassee children just before the school year started. My assistant coaches, players, and support staff at Florida State joined alongside 40 volunteers from Calvary Chapel at a Tallahassee housing project.

On a sticky August Saturday, nearly two hundred children showed up —typically tugging the hand or arm of the person that brought them—to receive a new pair of shoes, socks, and to have their feet washed. After some basketball drills, coloring, and testimony time, the children went to the washing station and that's when the uncertain faces started turning to bright smiles.

It's those expressions that make Samaritan's Feet what it is.

14

It is what separates Samaritan's Feet from other philanthropic organizations. While the children wait for their new pair of shoes, we have the opportunity to sit down, look each child in the eye, and wash their feet. Then we get to tell them why we're there. We have the chance to give the message of Christ's unconditional love and to tell them what Christ did for us on the cross.

That is what makes Samaritan's Feet so special. That's why it's significant. It's about more than socks. It's about more than shoes. Most of all, it's about washing feet.

Samaritan's Feet is about the hope that we have in Christ. As Christians, we're called to impact lives for God's Glory, and that is exactly what Samaritan's Feet does in a tangible, loving way. The opportunity to spread the message of hope to my program and the Tallahassee community was something I'll never forget.

ANDRÉ BAUER, LIEUTENANT GOVERNOR, SOUTH CAROLINA

Three years ago, I almost died in a plane crash. That event made me keenly aware that God had spared me because He had a greater purpose for my life.

My plane crashed on take-off because a handful of bolts used in overhauling the engine were one-quarter of an inch too small. This incredibly small detail led to the reality that the plane's airworthiness was compromised, which meant that it was able to lift from the ground but lacked the power to actually fly.

I felt that in many ways this was a metaphor for my life. Although most of my adulthood had been spent in public service, my lapses in judgment had diminished the perception of my efforts. As I accepted that small mistakes have big consequences, I realized that although God has lifted me, my choices had compromised my flight.

Through the pain of injuries and recovery, I focused on the knowledge and belief that God would send me opportunity for contrite service and redemption from my failures.

That's when I met a remarkable man who was blessed by God with a vision of accomplishing great things by small acts.

He was Manny Ohonme! His life in his homeland of Nigeria had been transformed by the gift of a pair of shoes.

Those shoes opened doors in that he became a basketball sensation who received a collegiate basketball scholarship in North Dakota.

From there, he found that as his success in the corporate world grew, so did the realization that God had a bigger plan for him.

Manny's vision is that he will find partners to give shoes to 10 million disadvantaged children. He has an unwavering belief that God has goals for each of them. Manny knows that every one of those children will be graced with as great an opportunity as God provided him. These children will transform the world to the glory of God.

As lieutenant governor of South Carolina, I stood barefoot with Manny in the rotunda of our majestic state house to announce that Samaritan's Feet would give up to 46,000 disadvantaged children in my home state the gift of a pair of shoes and hope for a better future.

Together, we have been blessed by energetic partners from the faith, education and non-profit communities as well as everyday people who have served as volunteers and donors. All our eyes have been opened by God to His joy that we are fulfilling this vision of many small acts transforming into major achievements.

As I provide this witness, it is with humble acknowledgment that we have made only a beginning in this ministry of service. Our successes are also humbling, as powerful men and women leaders kneel and wash the feet of small children as Jesus did for His disciples. A prayer flows from our hearts with the gift of shoes and socks. We pray that each small child will be inspired with the certain belief that God has a plan for maximizing that child's potential.

Each time, the words of the Gospel of Mark 10:14 spring into my mind: "Suffer the little children to come unto me and forbid them not, for of such is the kingdom of God."

All of us, those who wash the feet of these children and the little ones who until this day had largely been denied the fruits of the Blessing Tree, are swept up in Manny's vision. Greatness does rise out of little acts of service and gratitude. It is revealed in our hearts that "for of such is the kingdom of God."

PART 1

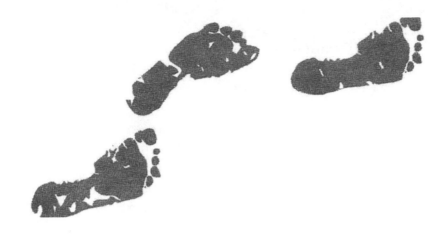

I: YES

In December 2007, I was invited to travel from Charlotte, North Carolina, to New York City to meet Thomas Kinkade, the famous "Painter of Light" whose work is displayed in tens of thousands of American homes. He was in New York to paint a portrait of the Christmas tree at Rockefeller Center, a painting that was to be reproduced as an art print. A portion of the proceeds from marketing that print would help support the charity I'd founded four years earlier, called Samaritan's Feet.

The unveiling of this painting was to coincide with the kickoff of a national campaign for Samaritan's Feet, designed to draw attention to our cause. We pledged to place 10 million shoes on the feet of 10 million children in 10 years' time, and we were trying to engineer some media opportunities to get our message out to the American public. Thomas Kinkade was scheduled to be on Fox News, where he was going to mention Samaritan's Feet, and talk about why he chose to work with a charity that distributed shoes to poor children around the world.

That was the primary reason why I traveled north with our head of marketing, Todd Melloh. It was why I had agreed to stand outside in the frigid temperatures of New York City that morning. Such cold isn't good for the bones of an African boy like me!

As it turned out, Thomas Kinkade forgot to mention Samaritan's Feet on Fox News that day. But there turned out to be a completely different and providential reason why God put us there in New York City at that particular time.

We met one of my favorite people, Dr. Maya Angelou.

The Gabarron Foundation had offered Dr. Angelou a lifetime achievement award for what she's done in poetry and the arts over her life, as well as for her powerfully positive impact on the African-American community. Todd and I got the chance to meet her right before that presentation, and it was a great honor to have a private audience with such a legendary woman.

I was born in Nigeria, and she told me that she had been there before. We even exchanged a few words in my native Yoruba language.

I asked her who her role model was.

"Dr. Martin Luther King," she replied.

"Why is that?" I wanted to know.

"Because every human virtue stems from courage," Dr. Angelou explained. "That man exhibited courage beyond that of an ordinary human being. Dr. King had the courage to use his platform to be a voice for people who didn't have voices."

Dr. King was killed on Maya Angelou's birthday, April 4, 1968. After he died, she went into a shell and withdrew from the world. She later dealt with her profound grief by writing the great and classic book, *I Know Why The Caged Bird Sings*.

She looked at Todd and I. Then she said to us, "Whatever it is that you are called to do, you must exhibit courage."

I was so inspired by that simple message. Todd and I attended her award presentation that afternoon, and watched as she shared the same message with the group. We were so excited that we had the opportunity to hear it before everybody else did.

We left the ceremony so motivated and pumped up! Todd and I went back to the New Yorker hotel, near Madison Square Garden. The hotel is across from the office I once had, when I worked in the corporate world. It had been my home away from home, but on that night it became the birthplace of an idea which set off a chain reaction that *changed the world*.

Todd and I sat in a hotel room at the New Yorker late that night. "What is something courageous that we could do?" we asked each other. "How can we honor the words of Dr. Angelou, the memory of Dr. King, and shine a spotlight on the plight of the 300 million children around the world who have no shoes?"

We went through all these different ideas, and almost all of them ended up in the trash bin. Nothing was good enough to stick.

At one point, Todd said, "What if we held a basketball game on national TV, where the teams would play in their bare feet?" He had a sports marketing background, and a lot of contacts all around the NCAA, NBA and NFL. He could call some people, he told me, and get something like that organized.

I shot that one down, like all the others. "That's not going to work," I said. "Players might get hurt, and playing in bare feet might violate the rules of basketball. I don't know if we could manage to get a league to go along with throwing out the rule book for a night!"

Some time went by, and Todd floated another idea.

"What if we could get a Division I basketball coach to coach a game in his bare feet?"

As soon as the words came out of Todd's mouth, I could sense that God was planting a seed of inspiration.

This one had merit. It was very visual, very powerful, and it tied in directly and perfectly with our mission. "Todd, that is an idea from heaven," I said.

There was only one question left: who was going to do this?

Todd responded, "Manny, there's a coach in Indianapolis. He's the head men's basketball coach at IUPUI."

"What in the world is that stuff?" I answered. "It sounds like a bad bowl of alphabet soup, man. I've never heard of that school before. IUP-who?"

"IUPUI," Todd exclaimed. "I know it sounds like a funny name, but it's the Indiana/Purdue joint university in downtown Indianapolis. There are 30,000 students who go to school there."

Thirty thousand? It certainly peaked my interest. "That's a lot of people," I exclaimed.

"But the thing about this guy... and I know this guy," Todd continued.

"He's willing to wear his faith on his sleeve, and never compromise."

I've got to meet this Coach Hunter from this crazy school with all the letters, I thought. I was intrigued.

"Let's call him right now," Todd said as he took out his cell phone.

"No, no, no, man, it's almost 11 p.m. It can wait until tomorrow."

Todd was adamant, and he started dialing. "We've got to strike while the iron is hot."

These days, people typically call other people's cell numbers. But not Todd, he was dialing up this basketball coach at home! Coach Hunter would later tell me that he was wondering who in the heck this was, calling him so late at night.

But Coach Hunter went ahead and picked up the phone. Todd was talking a mile a minute, he was so excited. Todd told Coach Hunter about Samaritan's Feet, about me, and he shared the story of what had happened that afternoon with Maya Angelou.

Then I talked to him. Todd and I just laid all this stuff on him, all at once. It got to the climax of the story, and then...

"Why are you calling me?" Coach Hunter asked. "What does all of this mean?"

"Coach," I said confidently. "You've been given an opportunity to be a basketball coach for a reason. We want to ask you to coach a basketball game on national TV in your bare feet."

There was dead silence on the line. I honestly thought he had hung up the phone. Those nine seconds that passed felt like an hour.

"*What!?!*"

"We want you to help us by coaching a basketball game in your bare feet," I repeated.

"My bare feet?" Coach Hunter echoed. There was another pause on the line. "Are you guys drunk?"

"Your life is going to change," we said to him. "It will change forever if you choose to be obedient to God and do this."

We arranged for me to meet Coach Hunter in person and talk more about this idea. I flew to Indianapolis 10 days later, and I remember when I walked into his office at IUPUI. Behind Coach Hunter's desk was one of the biggest framed posters of Dr. Martin Luther King I'd ever seen in my life.

"Coach Hunter," I said, pointing at the giant poster. "Without that man, you don't have a job at this institution. Do you realize what next year, 2008, is?"

"What is it?" he asked.

"It's the 40th anniversary of that man's death," I said. "It will have been 40 years since Martin Luther King, Jr. died on Maya Angelou's birthday. Would you help honor him, and honor all those children around the world with no shoes? Would you help us by coaching a basketball game in your bare feet, and will you also help us raise 40,000 pairs of shoes in honor of that man?"

"Manny, you are *crazy*," the coach shot back. "I thought for sure I'd like you when you came here, I thought I'd agree to raise, say, 500 or 1,000 or 2,000 pairs maximum. Then you lay this stuff on me?! You haven't seen my gym, it only seats 1,200 people! You're talking about raising 40,000 pairs of shoes?"

"Coach Hunter," I said. "If you can do 500 or 1,000, that's something *you* can do. But 40,000 is a God-sized number. You're going to need God to accomplish this task."

"I don't know if I can do this, man!"

"I'm not asking what you can and can't do," I replied calmly. "All I'm asking is for you to say Yes, and try. See what God will do in response to your obedience."

"OK, Manny. I'm going to try, but I don't know about all this..."

We put out the word, and it became a media storm that we never could have expected. We found that newspapers and television stations, ESPN and Fox, all wanted to broadcast the story of the barefoot coach in Indiana. Coach Hunter's phone was ringing off the hook with people wanting to interview him.

The school organized a Samaritan's Feet night on campus and asked students to go without shoes for the evening. Shoes poured in from everywhere. We reached 40,000 pairs of shoes, meeting the goal, and we just kept going past it. Converse pitched in, so did Nine West and Wal-Mart. By game day on January 24, by the time Coach Hunter coached that IUPUI-Oakland game in his bare feet, we had raised 110,000 pairs of shoes.

Look what God had done!

After the game that day, Coach Hunter was going to appear on ABC-TV's *Nightline*. But Charles Gibson read his story and decided, "No, no, we've got to make this guy Person of the Week."

And from that moment on, God *changed the game*.

That single and simple moment, when Coach Hunter removed his shoes and walked the sidelines in his bare feet, galvanized a global barefoot movement. Since then, thousands of basketball, football and track coaches have gone barefoot. Pastors have delivered their sermons without shoes on. Governors and state senators have gone barefoot to show solidarity to our cause. Later that year, I did a 300 mile walk from Charlotte to Atlanta in my bare feet. All these great things started happening, and millions of lives around the world were touched.

What a profound, powerful visual it is to go barefoot. It definitely gets people's attention, because shoes are such a symbol of fashion in this country. It's such an in-your-face statement. Walking a mile without shoes not only makes people really stand up and take notice, it is a humbling experience for the person taking those steps.

Going barefoot by choice causes others to pause. It's one thing to tell people that 300 million children around the world have no shoes, or that every 15 seconds a child dies from irrevocable disease, many of which are foot-borne. But it's another to walk that talk. It transcends language to feel how blistered and bloodied your feet become without the protection that shoes provide.

There are children in Kenya, on the other side of the African continent in Burundi, up in Nigeria and down in South Africa that have to wake up every morning and walk through dangerous terrain for four, five, six miles to fetch water. Their feet are their primary mode of transportation. They might step on thorns, nails, and corroded metal along the way. We've seen a lot of feet wrapped in dirty, filthy rags instead of shoes. Others wear makeshift shoes fashioned from plastic bottles or rubber tires. Some even use tar to protect the soles of their feet.

We all have a gift, and Coach Hunter's gift is to coach basketball. He realized an opportunity, and he used his platform as a Division I men's basketball coach to help change the lives of children in need. It was a selfless and generous act. It was also a painful act, because walking barefoot for a while isn't very much fun. When Coach Hunter went barefoot, it showed other leaders that they, too, can use the influence that they have to make a difference.

They can choose to say Yes, and help change the world.

NUGGETS OF VIRTUE

You may have heard this famous Mahatma Gandhi quote: "Be the change you want to see in the world." There is also a Chinese proverb attributed to Lao-tzu that says, "A journey of a thousand miles begins with a single step." To bring about real change, the process has to start somewhere, and it starts with you. It starts with "Yes." The decision to say "Yes" transforms you into an agent of change empowered to impact yourself, your community and your world.

The eye of the Lord is roving to and fro, looking for committed people He can trust with His vision. Are you willing to be a vessel that God can work through?

God is looking for two ingredients in each and every one of us. The first ingredient is our obedience, which begins with a bowed head: "Yes, Lord." We have to take that first step towards God, and that surrender to power represents the recognition that the journey's outcome cannot be controlled. But what we *can* control is our obedience, our willingness to yield to His will. The result is always up to God...this is the thing most people forget.

Regardless of your vision of whatever you feel called to do, remember not to take on the burden and yoke of responsibility. Give it to God. Obedience rests on us; it is our obligation. But the result belongs to the Lord.

His second request of us is our faithfulness. Faith creates the vessel and the vehicle that allows us to follow through to the end. A commitment to keep walking for the rest of those thousand miles is fueled by faith. For us to complete our mission, we have to know and believe that God is protecting our every step.

God will honor our obedience and faithfulness, rewarding us with supernatural results. Indeed, He will do supernatural things with or without us, so our success is not defined by our own terms. Utilizing these two virtues, He wants to accomplish great things through each one of us.

Every journey of obedience begins with Yes. Some of the greatest accomplishments in the history of this world began with that one word.

Two thousand years ago, the Lord of the universe came to earth in the form of a man. Jesus was willing to shed His royalty to become human, to say "Yes" to His father and die for a sea of sinful people. During His life on earth, He invested His heart in a motley crew of twelve fishermen, treasurers and accountants. He poured everything into those twelve vessels, and they chose to say "Yes" to the Master. And the Bible tells us that they went on to turn the world *upside down*.

I look at David, one of my favorite characters in the Bible. King Saul was shaking in his boots when he saw Goliath. But David, only a young man at the time, announced, "There is no way this Philistine will make a mockery of my God." David said "Yes" to the challenge and prayed that God would honor his obedience. And then, against all odds, he slung the stone and killed that giant. David's obedience and faithfulness made him one of the most unlikely heroes and one of the most successful kings in the history of the world.

Martin Luther King, Jr. was a man who wasn't going to let the circumstances or the status quo stop him; nothing was going to impact his ability to become the voice for civil rights and justice in this country. He said Yes. And he was willing to pay the ultimate price to impact change.

Rosa Parks was saying "Yes" when she uttered the words "no way." She spoke with conviction by placing herself in the wrong location at the right time. And "Yes" accomplished broke a barrier that changed society.

Nelson Mandela said Yes. He spent 27 years in prison, and as a free man he said "Yes" to forgiveness. He became one of the most powerful and influential leaders in Africa by instilling the ability to forgive into the fiber of future generations. He told his people to let go and let God. He chose not to allow bitterness to dictate his country's future.

Ron Hunter said Yes. He was a little-known basketball coach in Indiana who chose to coach a basketball game without shoes. Because of his Yes, hundreds of thousands of children around the world were blessed. Because of his obedience, thousands of public figures have walked alongside him: athletes from all sports, presidents and governors of nations. They chose to follow Coach Hunter's lead and remove their own shoes, to use their positions and platforms to be a voice for the voiceless. We have collected and distributed over 3 million pairs of shoes because one basketball coach said Yes.

In 2003, I said "Yes" to the Lord and started Samaritan's Feet. God honored my obedience and my faithfulness. Today, an organization that began in my own garage now works in over 50 countries.

God can use anyone to change the world. A man came to Africa almost 30 years ago, and he planted a seed of hope in the heart of an African boy. He said Yes. Now, millions of people have been touched because of the chain reaction set off by that obedience. And today, Christ's model of servanthood has been birthed: the richest of the rich are getting on their knees to wash the feet of the poorest of the poor.

What would America be like today if Martin Luther King, Jr. and Rosa Parks had not said Yes? Would others have stepped up in their places? Would there be another Mandela to inspire the youth of Africa if he had chosen vengeance instead? And what if Jesus Christ, if He had simply decided not to follow through with His mission? "These people don't care about who I am," He easily could have said. "I have no reason to sacrifice Myself for these ungrateful losers."

These are questions of unimaginable proportions. I know that I could have easily said No. I could have stuck with things I was familiar with. I knew how to make money in the business world. But I realized that I was given a call that was greater than me.

I do not know what would have happened if I had not said "Yes" to the Lord. Would there have been another Manny who would have realized this mission? What if a missionary had not given me my first pair of tennis shoes when I was nine years old? What if he hadn't said Yes?

What if my mother hadn't said Yes? What if?

2: DREAMS

My mother always told me, "I gave you to God even before you were born." There's a reason behind my name, why it is Emmanuel, which means "God is with us."

I grew up in Lagos, Nigeria. My mother was a first-generation Christian. My father's family practiced a traditional African religion; they prayed and sacrificed animals, and he blended and combined that with a little bit of Catholicism over time. In the animistic religion, the one my father's family practiced, there were people called medicine men, who claimed to do good in the community. But when others didn't follow along with what they said, they would cast spells and make sure that bad things happened.

Once my mother accepted Christ, she didn't subscribe to any of that nonsense any more. The way many of these medicine men operate is to spread fear into the community. And when people give into that fear, they're ordered to do all these sacrifices and rituals to protect them from evil things occurring. That's the way many of these types of religions operate in some third-world countries. They thrive off ignorance and fear.

When my mother was pregnant with me, a medicine man told her that the baby she was carrying was not going to be born unless she performed certain sacrifices. My mom simply smiled and replied, "You don't know my Jesus. I don't need to do any of that kind of stuff you're talking about. My child is going to be born, and grow up to be healthy and happy and serve the Lord."

My mom was one of the first individuals in our community who had enough courage to stand up to this medicine man.

"We're going to kill your baby, Florence Ohonme," the medicine man threatened. "Your baby is not going to live."

A few weeks before I was born, my mother had a very unusual encounter. She awoke from her sleep late one night and heard steps outside our two-room house in Lagos, coming through the main security door of our building, approaching our front door. These footsteps came closer and closer, and she could clearly hear the intensity of the steps through the walls.

My mom was a very brave woman and rarely got scared, but that night she became very frightened. She wondered, who was out there? At first, she thought it was my dad coming home.

My father, David Ohonme, was rarely home during those early times. He drank and partied a lot and always seemed to be gone when his first three children were born. But my mother called out, using the name by which she refers to him. "Dele," she said. There was no response.

She remembered something her pastor had once told her—that whenever she felt fear, she should call on the name of Jesus Christ. And his advice was in her mind in this critical moment. As the footsteps intensified, she summoned up enough confidence to cry out.

"Whoever is coming towards my door... in the name of Jesus, I command you to leave. Go away."

The steps that had once been drawing closer suddenly became fainter and fainter. They had turned around and left, headed back out into the dark of night. She heard the main door open, and then slam. The hair on the back of her head stood straight up on end!

When I was young, my mother told me that she made a pact with God that night. She prayed, "God, please save me from all this. Please allow me to have this baby, and if it is a boy, I will name him Emmanuel." (In Nigeria, as well as most of the countries in Africa, they didn't have the medical equipment for an ultrasound, so there was no way for her to know at the time if I was to be male or female.)

"I will name him Emmanuel," she promised God that evening. "'God is with us.' Because tonight, You were with me."

And when she gave birth, she kept her promise. When I was christened, she prayed, "God, I'm giving this child back to You to serve You."

Much later, when I left the corporate life to launch Samaritan's Feet, I called my mother and announced that I was going to choose to be obedient to the Lord—that I was saying Yes. When I told her I was going to dedicate my life to helping children around the world, you should have heard my mom scream for joy!

"I knew this day was going to come," she said through her tears.

To an outsider looking in, our household may have looked very poor, and while our family had to scrape by a lot, my mother made sure we never felt like we were poor or destitute. She always made us feel blessed.

She taught us about the power of giving and always said that it was important to give anything we didn't need to others, that we should give back to our community. In the morning, we often would only have a slice of bread, but by the end of the day, my mom made sure we had one great nourishing meal.

Most kids in my neighborhood often went without food, so we provided for others. At the end of the month, my mom went to the market to buy rice and beans and curry. We'd always take cups of our extra food to friends and neighbors who didn't have as much as we did.

I grew up in a cinder-block home with five sisters and my younger brother. When I was 11 years old, my first cousin Blessing's parents passed away, and he moved in with us. Our family took Blessing in as if he was ours, and the neighbors didn't even know for a while that he wasn't biologically linked to our parents. The only clue was that he was a little shorter than the rest of us—people would wonder if he'd just eaten some bad beans or something!

My father worked for the state parks and recreation department. My mom was a federal government employee who worked on the Nigerian census, and she was always trying to add to our household's income so we'd have what we needed. Many are surprised to learn that in most third-world countries, people are very entrepreneurial by nature, and my mom had a side business selling water and minerals (or soft drinks, as they're called in the west).

We lived near a sports complex called Rowe Park. She would buy cases of these minerals from the grocery store, then she and I, along with my sisters, would carry them over to the sports complex to sell. I might lug the bucket of ice, or help my mother with the cases. I was one of the vendors who would carry a few cold drinks on my head and run around selling them, while my mother handled the money. The extra cash helped us buy clothes or additional food.

Sometimes it was embarrassing, because a lot of my friends would be out there at Rowe Park playing sports. I look back at it now, and I remember that some of the other kids would poke fun at me. But somehow it was okay. I knew that I was doing what I needed to help my mom put food on our family's table.

Water was a scarce commodity in our area. We needed it to cook, to bathe ourselves, and to drink. So my sisters and I would walk for 45 minutes (or more at times) to fetch water with buckets and pails. Often, we would carry a tub all that way out to the water source, then try to get it back home without spilling it all on the road.

Our home had two bedrooms. My mom and dad slept in one room, and all the children stayed in the other. As my brothers and I grew older, we realized that my sisters needed privacy, so we boys started sleeping in the veranda and adjoining hallway. I slept on the floor for most of my childhood, and there were often rats crawling around because we didn't have adequate refrigeration to protect our food. When I was a junior in high school, I started sleeping on the table. I was moving up in the world, the cockroaches and I didn't have to see eye to eye at night anymore! When I was a senior I graduated to the couch; I thought I was the man. I finally had a little bit of padding on my back when I slept. .

When you live in the forest long enough, everything starts looking like a tree. Our home in dusty, dirty Lagos was the farthest thing from a literal forest, but fetching water and scraping by for extra food and sleeping on the floor was our way of life. But we were far better off than our relatives out in the village. They always wanted to come and stay with us and live the "high life," and they'd take over every little nook and corner of the house when they'd arrive for a visit.

My mother and father often fought. He heavily abused alcohol, and sometimes during my senior year in high school I'd find him passed out on the couch. He'd taken over my nice bed, and I'd have to crawl back on the floor to hang out with the bugs.

But sleeping on the floor was the least of my problems. The stresses of life weighed heavily on my father. In tough times, he always drew closer to the bottle and not the Lord. From my age 12 to 17, he was drunk almost every night. This was the time when I needed him most, when I was trying to figure out what adolescence was all about—when I needed a role model.

My father became a closet drinker during the latter part of my teenage years—he consumed his alcohol in the house instead of outside or in public. We saw everything up close and in person. And when my dad drank too much, this evil spirit would take over him. He'd swear and curse us out, and it would often become physical and violent. I'd always try to defend my mom during those fights, but that would always put me on his bad side and subject me to the brunt of his hatred.

There were moments I thought my mother was going to leave. But through it all, she kept praying for him.

My refuge during all of this was sports. I spent a lot of time at Rowe Park. I played basketball, because that was my safe haven where I was protected from my father's abuse.

I knew I had dreams in my head and heart. I knew I wanted to fly away from my childhood neighborhood. But I didn't know if those dreams were ever going to come to fruition. My mom never had the means to provide me that escape. However, she kept assuring me that God's plans always come to pass, no matter what. Our family did as well as we could under the circumstances, but luxuries were generally out of the question.

When I was nine years old, a group of sports-ministry missionaries came to Rowe Park. They were doing something similar to what Samaritan's Feet does today, acting as ambassadors for Christ in poor communities around the world. They came to play with us and run sports camps, to give us a few hours to help forget our impoverished state. They opened up a world of love, compassion, and grace.

A white person or a Westerner coming to our community would receive a lot of attention. Everybody wanted to be their friend. When these guys showed up, we wanted them to touch and hug us; we wanted them to look us in the eye. Even though there might have been a sea of people around them, each of us craved for just a few seconds of special attention.

They took an interest in each of our lives and made us feel valued, and we smashed the language barrier with laughter. For each child, that span of two hours was like the span of eternity for we felt like we were something we never thought we could become. When they held my hand, I'd go bragging to my friends. "A person from America touched me," I'd tell them. "He knows my name. I'm never washing this hand ever again!"

One of those missionaries was a man named Dave. He was from Wisconsin. Dave was organizing games and contests for us, and on that day I won a prize. That prize was my first pair of shoes. Canvas tennis shoes. I felt like a millionaire!

I had always gone barefoot; pretty much all the kids in my neighborhood did. We had no shoes. We walked barefoot, and we played barefoot. It didn't matter if the places we were walking and playing were smooth and paved, or if they were covered in thorns and broken glass—we never had a choice in the matter. When I first learned to play basketball, it was still without shoes.

But for a long time, I didn't even want to put my new shoes on. I was reluctant to get them dirty. I held onto them as if I was clutching two gold bars; those shoes were the most precious gift anybody had ever given to me in my whole life.

Then I grew bigger, and I got better at basketball, and my prized shoes started feeling really snug. My feet got so big that I had to curl my toes up so I could still stuff them inside those canvas shoes. But I didn't want to give them up. And in those days, we'd make sure whatever gifts we had would last as long as possible. Many times I would even take my shoes off, so I wouldn't wear them out by playing in them.

This simple pair of canvas shoes would alter the course of my life forever. Wherever Dave is now, he probably just regarded the gift as a random act of kindness. He had no idea that his precious act of compassion was a life-altering gift which changed the destiny of my life.

Some people call things like this happenstance, those God-like moments when He asks you to do something specific. We're hardly ever blessed with the full realization of all the ways God uses us as part of a greater plan, the knowledge of how we impact and show the world His love and who He truly is.

In retrospect, the greatest gift Dave gave me wasn't a pair of shoes. The real gift was the compassion those shoes ignited in me, when I saw the reaction on the faces of all the kids who didn't get any. I felt like I was blessed, but I also saw the sadness in the eyes of all the other kids who weren't as fortunate. I had two separate emotions competing for my heart: I was on top of the world with my new shoes, but what about all the others?

That to me was the real story of the day at Rowe Park... the children who didn't receive. Nowadays, if Samaritan's Feet came into a community and gave away only one pair of shoes, we wouldn't have many friends. This is the effect Dave and his friends could not have anticipated.

But at Samaritan's Feet, we never want anyone to feel left out. The need always outweighs the resources and the queues are endless, but I'm always trying to find a way to bless one more kid with shoes, to bless one last child. I do that because I remember the sad faces of my young friends that very day when I was only nine years old.

I graduated high school a year early, when I was 16 years old. I was a good student, one of the best in my class. But in Nigeria, the education system is very different than the one here in the United States. I always tell high school seniors in this country that they don't know how blessed they are to be Americans. Here, as long as your parents can pay for college or can secure sufficient loans, you can go to almost any university you want.

But in Nigeria, you must take and pass a test called the Joint Advanced Matriculation Board Exam. Your score determines which kind of university program you'll be accepted into and which level of study you'll be brought in at. Each university opens its gates for only a few hundred students, and thousands of applicants might apply for those spots! You might have the best grades in school, but if you don't know anybody in high places, or get a high test score, you're done for! I saw so many of the dreams of my friends die because of this system.

My dad wanted me to be a doctor, but he never put in the effort to help me get into a university. When I completed high school and wanted to get started in college, my board exam score was not high enough to get into medical school. It appeared that I was going to be one of those who fell through the cracks.

But I had one of the highest grade averages in my high school, so I had a good argument if I was able to take my case to the right people. If my dad, who worked for the state and had many connections, were to help me talk to the chancellor, I knew I'd at least get a shot.

But my father wouldn't connect me to any of the individuals he knew who might have come to my aid.

That's when my mom, God bless her, leapt into action. She took time out of work every day, and rode on buses with me to the universities, to go and see if they'd at least take a look at me. She thought that if I couldn't get into a medical program right away, there might be a chance I could do a one-year certificate cycle, which is a precursor for admittance into a main program. Chemistry is what I'd have studied first, a sort of a "pre-med" phase before medical school. This was the established process.

For the first few months, we visited many schools, but nothing was progressing. But then I finally was admitted to the pre-degree program at Lagos State University (LASU), and it was because of my mother's relentless, tireless effort. She'd always been there for me, and I must say that her insistence that I be admitted to the university was one of her finest hours.

At the same time, I was playing basketball and I knew I wanted to go to America to play there. My coach, Coach Ganiu, was also Hakeem Olajuwon's mentor. He took a lot of young basketball players under his wing, and this was the time when Olajuwon made basketball very popular in Nigeria. Coach Ganiu took a genuine interest in many young people. He set up mini-camps, got us into clubs, and always inspired us to stay involved in basketball.

He often traveled to America, and through his connections had numerous contacts to college coaches. He knew coaches at the University of North Dakota-Lake Region in Devils Lake, Nashville's Lipscomb University, Oklahoma Christian College (now Oklahoma Christian University), and Milligan College, to mention only a few.

Coach Ganiu sent them information about our talent, and he had us write letters of inquiry. Several responded favorably. A few even expressed a specific interest in me, based on what they read.

While I was going through pre-med school at LASU, I kept in touch with the colleges overseas. UND-Lake Region, Lipscomb University, and Oklahoma Christian all sent scholarship offers and Form I-20—which is what they give to international students.

Given all this interest, I didn't have a clue where to go. I was looking at all three of them, with the information they sent me spread out on the table at home. I didn't know Oklahoma from North Carolina from North Dakota... to me, America was America. I decided that I would go to the school with the best brochure!

So I picked UND-Lake Region. In their brochure, there were pictures of girls in a Corvette in the middle of summer, with the sun beaming down. I thought to myself, I'm going to this school, look at the beautiful-looking girls and the warm weather they have there!

(I wouldn't learn until much later that they had me fooled... I fell for that marketing ploy hook, line and sinker!)

I went to the embassy to apply for my visa, so I could travel to America and start college in North Dakota. They immediately rejected my application.

"I know you'll never come back to Nigeria if I let you go," the man at the embassy told me as he reviewed my passport. "So I'm not giving you a visa."

I was devastated.

It was as if my entire world had crumbled. In one definitive statement, this guy crushed my dream.

My best friend accompanied me that day; we took the bus together. When we got off at the station it was still a very long walk to the embassy. We had to arrive before 5 o'clock in the morning because so many people would be there. I finally made it into the office after many hours of waiting in line. They called my number. Then this guy, in one quick moment, ruined my dreams.

I walked out of the embassy, my friend saw my face and exclaimed, "Ohhhh, no. They didn't give you your visa, Tope, did they?" ("Tope" is the nickname my Nigerian friends referred to me by.)

Devastated, we jumped on the bus for the longest bus ride I've ever been on. Upon arriving home, I walked through our gate, through the door of our apartment, and my family saw me standing there. They saw the dejection on my face.

"Man, did somebody die or something?" my mom asked me.

"I'm not going to America," I told her. "They rejected my visa."

My mom pulled me close and whispered, "Son, do you believe that God wants you to go?"

"I hope so," I answered, very weakly.

"Then give it to God," my mom said. "Let Him take care of it."

I love my mom so much. She always encouraged me and my siblings and made anything possible. That day, she tried so valiantly to lift my spirits when I was so broken-hearted.

Later on, my mom had an idea. "I'm going to call my cousin Col. Macauley," she said. Her cousin (whom I call Uncle Macauley because he was also married to my dad's youngest sister) was a retired lieutenant colonel in the army. After retiring, he became the head of security for the Nigerian Airport Authority, an arm of the government that took care of all the international airports.

"I'm going to talk to him and see if there's anything he can do."

I remember praying with my mom for the next few days. We got down on our knees there in our apartment. "God, please open the window and pour your blessings in," we prayed. "We really need a favor, God."

My mom and I went to visit Uncle Macauley at his office. I told him what happened at the embassy, and he was furious. "Nobody dares kill my son's dream!" he raged.

He loved me so much that he called me his son. Uncle Macauley immediately phoned one of the people in the public relations office. "See to it that whoever rejected my son at the embassy makes this right," he ordered angrily.

Then he gave me a note. "Go back to the embassy. I'm going to call and let them know you're coming. Talk to this person, give him this note, and he'll make sure you are taken care of."

The name on the letter was that of the very same individual who had previously rejected my visa.

I went back to the embassy with my best friend the very next day. I stood in line just like I had the first time. I walked into the office, and I showed the man at the desk the letter Uncle Macauley had given me. And let me tell you, I may have been a nobody from a cinder-block house, but this guy treated me as if I was the son of the king!

This time, everything was different. "Oh! You want to go to America!" he exclaimed. "You're going to love it over there!"

I was flabbergasted. I thought, is this guy for real? Was this really the same person? Was this the same individual who had killed all my hopes and broken my heart just a short time earlier? It couldn't possibly be!

"It's such an incredible country, so many wonderful things to see!" he rattled on as he looked over my passport. "New York! Chicago! The Grand Canyon! Don't you worry, we're going to process this right away. Have you ever been to America before?"

"Ummm, no," I answered, completely shocked out of my mind. "I thought you knew that. You just rejected my visa a few days ago!"

I came out of the embassy's department for non-immigrant applicants, and you would have thought I was floating in the sky! My legs were completely out from under me. I was flying!

I was so excited I couldn't contain myself. And then they called my number, and gave me my beautiful new visa. Oh MAN! I jumped so high. I yelled out, "Lord, have mercy!"

My buddy, who was waiting outside, expecting the worst, saw my face as I walked out of the embassy.

"Yes!" he cried out as he ran to give me a congratulatory hug. We were both over the moon.

I was on my way. I was going to America!

I walked through our security gate, through the door of our apartment, and my family saw me standing there. I was wearing the biggest smile in the whole world. They knew. This brother was on his way!

And then reality hit... that's always the difficult part of any dream. When you realize the dream is possible but there is a seemingly impossible barrier standing in your way. My parents didn't have enough money to send me to the United States.

As heroic as my mother had been up until now did not prepare me for what she was to do next. My mom sold just about everything she owned. I'm not kidding. She sold nearly all her earthly possessions just to make my dream come true.

She talked to some of my uncles and our family friends, and borrowed money to raise enough cash to buy my plane ticket. I will never truly know how she put those funds together, but my dear mother wanted to see my dream come true. Because of her tremendous sacrifice, she was able to buy the ticket for me.

She also handed me $300 in spending money, for emergencies and whatnot. To Nigerians, $300 is a ton of money. At that time, it represented almost six months of my mother's income.

My father, on the other hand, didn't want me to go to the United States, and he didn't want to have any part of it. I remember the day I left, we had a big party. It was the happiest day of my life, and my dad wasn't even part of that special moment with me. As I celebrated with my mother and sisters, he was sitting in the courtyard with his drinking buddies. When we left for the airport, he didn't even say goodbye or get up to congratulate me. He didn't offer a hug or tell me, "Son, I'm proud of you."

My father just sat there and predicted, "You'll never make it."

"You don't *dare* say anything like that to my son," my mom told him sternly.

I found out later that he confided to his friends, "He won't really go. He's not serious about this."

So he was utterly shocked when my mother and sisters returned from the airport and realized that I was actually gone. He couldn't believe that I had truly left Nigeria for the United States.

NUGGETS OF VIRTUE

One of the greatest weapons that God has given to humanity is the ability to dream. This is what separates humans from every other created being on earth. Dreams give us the potential to envision the impossible, and to visualize the inconceivable.

What seems impossible to man is always possible to God. Even though at first a dream might feel as far away as the moon, you have a heavenly Father who knows you by name, who knows your thoughts, and sees every single tear that drops from your eye. He always hears you when you call.

This is why I always remind children to dream, and to dream big. This is what keeps hope alive; it's the art of removing all negative expectations from your mind. When you look at the acronym of "hope," those letters stand for "Have Only Positive Expectations." And regardless of what you might be going through right now, you can choose to hope. If you have this perspective on life, I believe you will become a winner and be successful —even when your circumstances spell out otherwise.

I think the most difficult and challenging battle anyone will ever fight is waged between their two earlobes. The only way to gain an edge in that battle is when one chooses to go beyond the physical, and operate in the spiritual realm. In the physical world, a lot of things make absolutely no sense. For instance, how could a poor Nigerian boy from a third-world country ever come to America and be a success? How could that boy grow up and impact millions of children's lives around the world? These are things for which there are no scientific explanations or physical laws.

These are the fruits of dreams.

The Lord is always looking for vessels who He can operate through. The question is: are we available? Can we be a conduit that the Almighty can trust with His vision? As long as we harbor hope in our hearts, as long as we can believe that our God is the God of endless possibility, our dreams can and will come true.

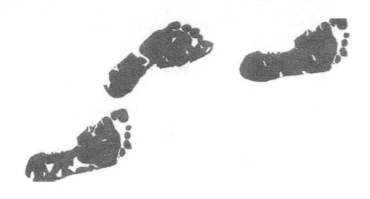

3: DETERMINATION

I flew from Lagos to Rome on Air Italia, then waited for 12 hours for my connecting flight to Chicago. I simply didn't realize that these planes wouldn't get me all the way to North Dakota. I just assumed the ticket my mother had purchased would get me to where I was going.

I had no concept whatsoever of how huge America really was.

When I arrived at O'Hare Airport, I retrieved my bags from the luggage carousel. I then asked some strangers the way to North Dakota, and I showed them a scrap of paper upon which I'd written the address.

"Oh, son," they told me. "You've got a long way to go."

"What do you mean?" I innocently asked.

"North Dakota's a long, long way from here," was the reply.

We Nigerians can get pretty much anywhere we need to go by bus. I was told about a service called Greyhound, but I found out that it was going to take me almost two days to get to my final destination. Holy smokes, I thought, how far away is this place? How big is this country, anyway?

A very kind lady at an information desk told me about Northwest Airlines. "Northwest will get you there," she assured me. So I got into the line at the ticket counter.

"Where are you going, son?" the lady at the counter asked me. I showed her the address: Devils Lake, North Dakota.

She informed me the closest airport was in Grand Forks, and that there was a flight leaving in two hours. And then she told me the price: $180.

I was exasperated. "180 dollars! All I have is $300!"

The money I had in my pocket was all my family had raised for me. My mother sold everything to help me get to America, and I thought that these funds were going to last me for a year, and hopefully longer than that!

"Just let me know what you want to do," said the ticket agent.

I tried to be shrewd. "Isn't there any type of discount you could give me?" I asked. "Isn't there any way you could help me out?"

"Discount!?"

This was my first lesson that there is definitely no free lunch in America! This was a same-day ticket, cash and carry, no discount.

I did the math in my head, I'd only have $120 left if I bought this ticket... and how was I going to survive in a country where the prices were like this? I thought about what it entailed for my family to scrape that much money together. It took them almost four months. And here I was, spending over half of it within an hour of my arrival in America!

I was pacing back and forth. "If you want to get on this plane, you've got to purchase the ticket now," the agent said.

So I finally bought that ticket. Lord have mercy, I thought. Two hours later, I boarded the plane, and we were delayed on takeoff.

Being Nigerian, I didn't think to call ahead. Nobody calls ahead in Africa, people just show up! So I didn't phone anyone to tell them I was on my way.

When I landed in Grand Forks, I called my basketball coach on the telephone. Nobody was home. What's up with this? I thought to myself. Doesn't he know I'm coming?

I actually thought they would be waiting around for me! I called a few times, and still there was no response. I found out later he was away traveling in Phoenix, Arizona, playing golf.

Once I learned more about America and knew what Arizona was all about, I realized why he wanted to be in Phoenix instead of in North Dakota. It was so cold in that airport, colder than I'd ever been before in my entire life. And I was wearing a linen suit, I was definitely not prepared to have my bones frozen.

I went to the counter, and they told me that the last bus of the day to Devils Lake had already departed. There was a Hertz rental car outlet at the counter, and the young guy there told me that he could rent me a car. I guess he just assumed I had a driver's license!

I looked at him and explained, "Hey buddy, I'm from Africa! I don't even know where I'm going!"

"No problem," he said. "We have a detailed map we can give you."

"Brother," I answered him with a big laugh. "We don't know about these kind of directions where I come from. You walk about five or ten minutes until you reach a tree, then take a right. That's what we call directions in Nigeria! I don't know how to look north, south, east, or west!"

He finally relented when he realized he couldn't rent me a car, no matter how much he wanted to help me out.

So I slept in the airport that night. The security guard let me curl up on a chair and nap there.

And that was my first day in America.

I walked out of the terminal the next morning. Across the street was a Hardee's restaurant, and this was my first experience with an American fast food chain. I longingly looked up at that big red sign.

I'd been dreaming for months about eating a real American burger. When I went inside, I began looking at the pictures on the menu, just salivating.

But I had this thick accent, so it was hard for them to understand what I was ordering. All I knew to say was, "I want a hamburger." I didn't know there was a difference between a hamburger, a cheeseburger, a quarter pounder with cheese, a triple-stacked burger, all of that. So I ordered a hamburger, and was brought this flimsy little patty on a bun. I looked at it in dismay and said, "No, no, this isn't what I ordered."

"You wanted a hamburger!" the waitress responded.

"I wanted the *big* burger," I replied, spreading my hands wide. The staff just looked at me sideways, like, what's up with this African boy?

I'd learn later on that I had to order what I wanted based on the pictures on the menu, but this was just too much information for my boggled mind to process. I finally just gave up and said as clearly as I could, "Don't worry about it. Just give me another hamburger."

I also learned what the price of those two hamburgers was. I performed calculations in my mind. Once I did the currency conversion to Nigerian nairas in my head, I thought, holy smokes, this food is expensive! There was no way in the world anybody would spend that much money on food back home.

My money was quickly disappearing, and it was originally supposed to last me a long time. I knew I couldn't make hamburgers a habit.

I paid for the food, went over to the Greyhound bus station, and boarded the first bus of the day. The driver told me it was only 90 miles from Grand Forks to Devils Lake. But it took us over four hours, and I'm not kidding! The bus stopped in every little town along the way. How far away was this place?

When I finally arrived in Devils Lake, it was freezing cold, even more frigid than Grand Forks. But I had three more miles to get to campus. Since I didn't call anybody, no one had made arrangements to meet me. So when I stepped off that Greyhound bus, I asked someone at the depot how to get to UND-Lake Region. "Just go out the door, take a left, go straight, and you'll run into it," they told me. It was far too cold to run, so I started walking.

The saving grace for me was that the local newspaper had published an article about my arrival in town. Because of that story, people in the town knew there was a guy named Emmanuel from Nigeria who was on his way. And as I walked out onto the main street, a family was driving along and saw me, this African guy in a suit with all this baggage, walking in the cold.

They must have thought, "Hey, this poor guy's lost. He's obviously not from around here." I was definitely the only 6-foot-4 African brother on that street right then! They pulled over and rolled down the window.

"Where are you going?" they asked me.

I answered happily, "I'm going to college!"

"Hop in, we'll give you a ride."

North Dakota people are some of the most genuine, kind and compassionate folks I've ever met, and I had just met the Mosers, a family that would become my friends for life. This family ended up adopting me as their own son when I attended school in Devils Lake.

"We knew you were coming, we read about you in the paper," Sheila Moser, a woman I'd eventually call my "mom," said to me. "We're so glad you're here!"

They drove me to campus, but nobody was there. It was the weekend, and so everybody had left.

"Do you want to come home with us?" they asked.

So I went home with these total strangers! I was hungry and so exhausted from my journey. Sheila made stuffing and mashed potatoes and all this great American food. She baked rolls that were so delicious, she still sends me some to this day. So here I was, sitting at their table. We prayed, and started eating.

But I didn't know how to eat this food, this stuff was different from what I was used to! All of a sudden, everyone stopped eating and started staring straight at me. I asked, "Oh no, what am I doing wrong?"

I had cut open my roll and was filling it with stuffing, like I was eating a stuffing sandwich! Everyone was looking at me with huge, wide eyes—what was this guy doing? I was eating like I was never going to have another meal in my life! Really putting it away.

After supper I was cold, tired, and mentally wiped out. The Mosers told me I could sit down on the couch, but I fell asleep instantly.

When I awoke, Larry, Sheila, and their sons were gone. There was nobody else in the house but me. Wow, I thought, what am I doing here? These people had only known me for a few hours, but they trusted me and left me alone in their house!

In Lagos where I grew up, *nobody* would dare let a stranger be alone in their home. All their belongings would be gone when they got back! So it was overwhelming to me that this family had given me so much trust. They left a note, letting me know that they had to go out and would be back soon. I could help myself to anything in the fridge, the note said.

I thought to myself, my gosh, people in America are so trusting!

I fell in love with this family, and they embraced me. Larry and Sheila and their three sons (Brett, Marco and Kelan) came to every one of my basketball games to cheer me on. They all attended my graduation. They loved on me all the time, and we'd go to family camp together every year. The Mosers have been a huge blessing in my life ever since I arrived in America, and I still speak to them often. I call their three sons my brothers. They were young schoolboys in the car that day they picked me up, but now they've grown up to be men. Brett and Marco are married, and Kelan is currently engaged.

When my coach came back from Phoenix, he arranged a housing situation for me on campus. He put me in a room that had a window so I could see outside.

I told him, "You don't understand, I don't want to see that cold, white stuff on the ground out there." So the residence hall advisors moved me.

In this dormitory, there was a room against the far wall on both sides, then there was a section in the middle. This section was a storage area, sort of a quasi-boiler room. And I moved in there. I didn't want a window, I had no desire to look outside and be reminded that I was in a land with all that snow.

I received my first-ever bed! I'd never slept on a bed until I came to America. And because I was given a double room, I put the two beds together to make it king-sized. For two months I only ventured outside when it was absolutely necessary. I delighted in lying on my back on my very own bed. The room was 86 degrees because it trapped all the heat inside, and it was like a little piece of Africa.

I thought I'd died and gone to heaven! I had my own room with my own bed.

I was so excited and couldn't wait to call home and tell everybody everything. I'd spent my entire childhood sleeping on tables, couches and the floor. I now had a bed and I'd really arrived.

I was living large!

I didn't forget the vehicle that brought me to America in the first place: my basketball talent. My style was very physical, which is how we played in Nigeria. I was a 6-4 power forward, which is a position usually played by people who are much taller, but my physicality and athleticism made up for the size gap. And I learned one thing very quickly: the African style of basketball is very different than the American kind. These boys in the U.S. run fast!

My basketball coach was named Terry Porter. He wasn't the former Portland Trail Blazer player, this was the white version of Terry Porter. He actually looked like former Lakers and Heat coach Pat Riley, and our whole team always gave him a hard time about that. And those two years on the UND-Lake Region basketball team were some of the best times of my life. We could never go outside because it was so cold, but in the gym I encountered some of the warmest hearts I ever met. They treated me like gold.

I remember meeting my new teammates. Some of the players were from North Dakota, others from Texas, Wisconsin, and Iowa. Before I arrived on campus, the team had gotten together and purchased a surprise gift for me. Each had made a contribution and bought me my first boom box! I was just so touched by their generosity that I kept that boom box for a long time. In fact, I still have it in my attic at home.

I was taking 32 credits and was a very good student. After all, I'd graduated from a Nigerian high school a year early, at the age of 16. But at this college, I found the education so easy, I never had to study hard at all. In my two years at UND-Lake Region, I received both an associate of arts degree and an associate of applied science.

So with all the time I didn't spend studying, I did everything I could around campus. I was a residence hall leader, a basketball player, served in the student legislature, and went to the state capital at Bismarck as part of a student government group. I even served on the national residence hall committee, and they sent me to Emporia, Kansas for a convention. Everyone on campus thought I was crazy for doing all this extra-curricular stuff!

But the people in Devils Lake loved this crazy African boy. I was always receiving invitations to speak in the community, and tell people about my experiences growing up. I was invited to their homes for the holidays, for the weekends too. Everybody wanted me to come over and meet their families. I got close to many wonderful individuals in that town, and a lot of them are still good friends of mine.

There were two other black players on our basketball team. One of them was always complaining about racism on campus and in the town. "Everyone's always out to get us," he kept saying. "Coach Porter is so racist, he never plays me. And all these white people around here, they keep looking at me sideways. It's like they're expecting me to steal their money or something."

The other one was a dear friend of mine, but he was constantly getting in trouble. He would get drunk, or they'd find him sneaking into the girls' dorm, or doing something else that broke the rules. He was having problems with the administration, a couple of times he almost lost his scholarship. "Manny," he would complain to me. "Ever get the impression you're being singled out because you're black?"

"I don't know what you guys are talking about," I'd reply. "I don't see this racial problem you keep grumbling about."

"Aww, you're just African," they'd tell me. "We're African-*Americans.*"

I always gave them a hard time about that statement. "I think you've got to look at the mirror a little bit closer and see what's staring back at you," I'd advise. "Maybe you guys are the source of the problem."

But I almost let those players talk me out of staying in North Dakota. I kept hearing all these negative words from them, and I wasn't getting much playing time as a freshman. Coach Hayes at Oklahoma Christian was who I originally wanted to play for, because of the very strong interest he showed in me when I was back in Nigeria. But that was before I made a last-minute decision to come to UND-Lake Region, based totally on that brochure with the pretty girls and the Corvette.

When I arrived in Devils Lake, it finally dawned on me that they had either taken that picture in July—or used some very good trick photography!

So for a while, I thought about transferring to play for Coach Hayes.

Thankfully, I came to my senses. I realized I had to accept my role, stay positive, and remain free of distractions. Our team had its ups and downs, and it wasn't until my sophomore year when I really blossomed. Everything clicked that second year.

When I was a freshman, the girl who would eventually become my bride was a senior at a local high school. A lot of the kids who came to our college had attended this high school, so I knew who Tracie was. I didn't really know her personally, I just knew that she was one of the pretty cheerleaders for the basketball team, and I saw her at some of our home games.

In my sophomore year, I really made headway as a basketball player. Then the student government sponsored me to enter the running to become the "king" for the school's version of homecoming in February. They called it Sno-Daze, and it was a big deal on campus. There was a Sno-Daze dance, and to top it all off, a royal Sno-Daze court was presented. There was a big voting process beforehand, and there were always five or six candidates for each position.

Lo and behold, in my second year, UND-Lake Region had its first-ever Nigerian Sno-Daze king!

Everybody had gathered in the gym for the announcement, and the place erupted when they called my name. I knew a lot of people liked me, but I didn't know they liked me *that* much! The applause and the love they showed was simply overwhelming... it was all so awesome.

At the Sno-Daze dance, I asked Tracie to dance with me. She was working on campus in the library as well as at a restaurant in town. I still didn't really know who she was, so I asked her name while we were on the dance floor. Tracie was so pretty; she was tall and skinny with long blonde hair.

From February until the end of the school year, I would hang out in the library pretending I was doing my homework. I was always checking out a whole bunch of books I didn't need. She eventually figured out this Manny character was either a really good student, or just checking *her* out.

But you know I was getting really smart from studying that gorgeous-looking girl!

We'd make light conversation. "Hello, how are you doing?" "I'm great, how about yourself?" I'd see her around town and kept wanting to ask her out on a date, but nothing really moved in that direction. At first, I was more than a little bit shy around Tracie.

Then it was April, and time for the annual end-of-school dance. I asked Tracie to dance with me again. "I know you, Manny," she said, smiling. "You're the Sno-Daze king. I see you in the library all the time... it seems like you're always there."

And I was thinking, man oh *man*, this girl is beautiful. Lord, please let her be mine!

Tracie and I danced, and after the event was over I asked if she wanted to talk for a while. As I got to know her even more, I asked her if she wanted to go to a movie.

We went on our first date, but we never made it to the movie. We just hung around the student union, and talked for hours on end. That eventually turned into a second date, and we finally ended up going to the movies. But honestly, I don't remember what the name of the film was! I spent the whole time thinking about how I was going to get that girl to kiss me on the lips.

Our courtship was amazing. We'd talk together for hours about our lives and our dreams. She was so supportive and always took care of me. She also made sure I ate well by fixing me up with food from the restaurant she worked at. But then the time came for me to transfer out, because UND-Lake Region was a two-year school. I was really conflicted, because I finally found someone I truly liked, and suddenly I had to leave campus.

I wanted to feed kids in Africa, that was my dream at the time. I knew what it was like to go hungry. A lot of kids in my neighborhood only had one meal a day, so I wanted to study agriculture so I could help provide food for poor kids back home. I thought I was going to end up working with the United Nations or some similar organization.

So during my first two years at UND-Lake Region, I worked towards an agriculture business degree. I wanted to learn how to grow and market crops. Then I wanted to layer international relations on top of that, so I could add some political skills to my arsenal.

Concordia College in Moorhead, Minnesota, had the only international relations degree program in the north central United States. It was a small private university, and I didn't want to go to a large city college. Sharon Etemsad, president of UND-Lake Region, had a cousin named David who was an alumnus of Concordia, and he took me there to tour the campus. I met the basketball coach, and the school gave me a scholarship. Concordia doesn't give full basketball scholarships, but my two-degree performance at UND-Lake Region was good enough to get me in on the basis of my academics. Which was a good thing, because this college was as expensive as could be!

I thank God that I have been blessed in every environment I've been placed in. I have enjoyed great friends and phenomenal connections. I loved the Concordia campus, the people, and I was living in a beautiful apartment off campus. I also loved the fact that the school had a really tight-knit alumni group. I still stay in touch with a lot of the professors who taught me. I could go back tomorrow, and I'm sure the love would still be there.

But the tough part of transferring to Concordia was that Tracie was three hours away. She was in her second year at UND-Lake Region, and so we carried on a long-distance relationship. Almost every weekend, I'd drive that stretch from Moorhead to Devils Lake.

At the time, I was driving a cream-colored 1982 Toyota Tercel. It didn't even have a working radio, so we had to bring along a boom box if we wanted to listen to music. Any time we went on the interstate and a semi tractor-trailer passed us, the whole car would shake. I'd be scared out of my wits!

Once, when I drove her back home after a visit, there was one of the worst blizzards I encountered during my time there. The snow drifts were 12 feet high, the visibility was less than a quarter mile—I only had tire tracks to guide me, and I couldn't see the road. I was so tense trying to get her home alive.

I said to myself, "Man, what am I doing in this frozen north?"

After Tracie finished her second year at UND-Lake Region in June, she moved so that she could be closer to me. Fargo is just over the Minnesota-North Dakota border from where Concordia is, so we didn't have to endure those treacherous drives anymore.

I remember taking her to one of the parks in Moorhead one summer afternoon. I took her there with a secret ulterior motive. At one point, as I was pushing her on the swing, I took a ring from my pocket and knelt down beside her, and that's when I asked her to be my bride. She informed me later that after we'd been dating for three months, she told her mother that I was the guy she was going to spend the rest of her life with.

Tracie never thought she would ever get married. Her parents went through a painful divorce, and she didn't want to have anything to do with marriage. But God, in His providence, brought a guy all the way from Nigeria into her life to completely rock her world and change everything.

We both have come from super humble beginnings (and horrible automobiles) to where we are today. As I write this, we've been married for over 16 years and have four lovely children. We are both dedicated to each other and to the Lord and our journey together has just been phenomenal.

On the basketball court, things weren't quite so happy. The coach at Concordia used a different system than I'd become used to at UND-Lake Region. He had his own ideas about rotations, about how he used his players. The thing that frustrated me was that there were three African-American players on the team, including myself, and none of us played. Finally, all three of us made the decision to quit at the same time.

It didn't have anything to do with racism at all, it was just that none of us fit the style of play the coach preferred. There was a lot of standing around, setting up plays for shooters, similar to a Princeton type of offense. If you were a good shooter, you saw a lot of playing time. But if you were a more athletic or physical player, you sat on the bench for the whole game. This style wasn't working out very well; the team had a .500 record all through the season, and teams with better athletes would run all over us. We weren't great by any stretch of the imagination.

I quit because I hated being on the bench. I couldn't stand spending games sitting in my warm-up sweats, not being able to get in there and help my team.

But the irony is that I became a better basketball player after I left. I looked at my skills after I stopped playing on the team, and I measured them against the quality of the players I was playing pick-up games with afterwards. I finally realized that if I'd played one more year, I could have been a *great* basketball player. In retrospect, I wish I had asked my coach to redshirt me for a year, and to let me come back later to play instead of allowing me to walk off the team.

But I was so focused on my goals that basketball was just a tool to get me there. Basketball never defined who I was.

There's a word that Tracie always uses to describe me: determined. Nobody can tell me what I can't do, and when people make the mistake of telling me I can't accomplish something, it always fuels me to finish that job. Quitting basketball was the only time I let go of my determination to succeed. When I look back, not playing that fourth year of basketball was one of my main regrets in life. If I could do it all over again, I would have done that part differently.

My determination manifested itself in other ways. I ran track—my events were the indoor 55 meter dash, the 100 meters, and the long jump. Volleyball was a winter scholarship sport for women at Concordia, but a non-sanctioned spring club sport for men. I was the top player on our club team, drawing from my experience playing that sport back in Nigeria. As a child, I had played volleyball (barefoot, of course) before I really got into basketball. Our team played in a number of different tournaments, and the competition was fierce.

I had set many goals for myself, and was so driven. I told myself that by the time I was 30 years old, I would be a millionaire. Nothing was going to stop me or get in my way.

I used Concordia as a doorway to enter the next chapter of my life, and I wanted to get out of college as quickly as I could. I doubled my course-load and graduated with my bachelor's degree in December 1992. If I'd stayed on a normal schedule, it would have taken me until the second semester in 1993 to finish up.

After graduating from Concordia, Tracie and I got married on the second day of January. We really wanted to tie the knot on New Year's Day, but I received some sound advice from a friend. "Manny, seriously. Do you want to be the only guest at your wedding?"

In North Dakota, these people like to *party*. They're liable to oversleep into the afternoon after a long night on New Year's Eve!

Even though there was a bad snowstorm the night before our big day, a lot of people came from far and wide to Devils Lake to see Tracie and I become husband and wife. It seemed the entire town showed up for our wedding; it was a packed house.

Our friends from college were there, plus basketball players from UND-Lake Region and Concordia. A friend of mine from Romania drove in from Minneapolis and almost got himself killed in the storm, but thankfully he arrived safely. My rancher friends and Native American buddies from Halliday, North Dakota came too—I was spending every May living the old-school cowboy lifestyle, riding horses and branding cattle with them. Chad Dahlen, one of my best friends and the owner of that ranch, brought his entire family and served as my best man.

The wedding was phenomenal. I had six men in my wedding party, six of Tracie's friends accompanied her. We were married at the church where Tracie truly gave her heart to Christ, after "punching the clock" at church for years as a "non-committed" Catholic.

I remembered how when we started dating, we agreed that our spiritual life was going to have to be an important part of our journey. I started bringing her to the church I was attending in Devil's Lake. She loved me, so she came. Even when I left that community, Tracie kept going to the church. Pastor Cliff Close was married to an African-American lady from Kansas City named Millie, so he was part of an interracial couple too. There were a lot of reasons why it was powerful and emotional to have him officiate our ceremony.

It was a happy day, but at the same time it was tinged with sadness. Even though we were surrounded by loving friends, it was very difficult for me because I had no biological family present. My parents were unable to come because I couldn't afford to buy plane tickets for them. One of my adopted brothers, who lives in Seattle, was going to represent my family by proxy, but he got stuck in the storm. So the Mosers, the family who had been there for me the day I first arrived in Devils Lake, stood in for my family. The gift that Larry and Sheila and their three sons provided, I will never forget.

Even though the ceremony was so emotional, many were dismissive of our chances. They doubted our marriage was going to last. Some of our friends thought our courtship was just a phase for both of us, and it was a surprise to many when we decided to get married after just two years of dating.

It was a different type of racial mentality in North Dakota in those days, a state that has always been overwhelmingly Caucasian. People there wouldn't say a lot, but they'd stare like crazy. If looks were weapons, Tracie and I would have been blown away by M-16's! Strangers on the street would stop dead in their tracks and stare us down. I'm glad that things have changed a lot in North Dakota since then.

After she moved to Fargo, Tracie and I attended church, and the marriage counselor there was trying his hardest to discourage us from getting married. He put us through a personality test, and we overlaid each other's profiles perfectly—according to this test, we were a dream match. But Brad kept asking us, "Do you know what's going to happen to your children? You guys really need to think through the interracial aspect of this."

"Pastor Brad," I said. "This is God's plan for our life. Who are you to tell us what to do and what not to do?"

"I'm just concerned about your future," he insisted. "I'm worried about the future of your children."

"Thank you for your concern," I replied. "But we're getting married as long as it is part of God's plan for our lives."

I was very fortunate that I was able to combat perceptions and stereotypes in my time there. Racism stems from ignorance, from not knowing. However, I attempted to make people feel comfortable, regardless of their skin color. Most of my friends were white because there just weren't very many African-Americans in that frozen land.

And it didn't help matters that some among the small number of African-American friends in the Fargo-Moorhead area were very promiscuous; having children out of wedlock. A lot of concerned parents didn't want their daughters hanging out with African-American guys, thinking that they would get their daughters pregnant. So we would often be pre-judged before the local people really knew our character and who we were.

I was an anomaly. I knew what I wanted and was totally focused on my goals. I was determined to make my dreams a reality. But I had to work a little harder to make people see that because of my relationship with the Lord, I wasn't like the others. My nature has always been to love everybody, and I would never let anyone pre-judge me on the basis of race. I would strive to find the right things to do and say in order to win people over.

For the longest time, my father-in-law would make negative comments about blacks... forgetting I was in the room. I'd say, "Dad, what do you think *I* am?"

John, Tracie's stepfather, was a truck driver. He'd been robbed on the road by both whites and blacks, but he had a negative stereotype and prejudice against African-Americans earlier in our relationship.

I remember my first visit to Tracie's home when we were dating. That must have been the best and the worst day of her dad's life. He didn't know whether to jump for joy, cry, or embrace me. He didn't know what to do. Oh my goodness, he must have thought. What did Tracie just bring home?

But there wasn't much he could say or do about it. Her mother married John when Tracie was 14, and he had limited authority over her. He couldn't always tell her what to do.

"Manny, I don't know how to take this," John said to me on this first visit. "I know everybody in this town loves you, but this is my daughter we're talking about."

I found out later on that John had gone and sought counsel from an African-American guy in Grand Forks, a mechanic who worked on his truck. He knew this mechanic was married to a white woman.

"I don't know what to do," he told him. "My daughter is dating an African man."

"Let me give you some advice," came the reply. "If you won't embrace him, you're going to lose your daughter. She's going to follow her heart and do what she wants to. It's up to you whether you become a part of this, or look in from the outside."

John finally came around and accepted me. "I love Tracie too much to lose her," he told me one day. "I don't want to do anything that will break the heart of my daughter. I'm willing to try. Just promise me that you will never mistreat her."

I respected John for saying that. And I happily made my promise.

"Because if you don't take care of my daughter, I'm going to take your head," John added, smiling and laughing.

In addition to starting a family, I was working on building a resume. After I graduated from Concordia, I joined the campus police force at the college. That was a job and a half. There were guys who at that time partied on and off campus, and they'd recognize me from the basketball team. "Hey, Manny, what's up? Looking good in that uniform!"

On top of this, a lot of people I knew from class were still students there because I had graduated early. Some would break rules, and here was their old friend coming to bust them! I'd gone from a buddy to "the man" overnight, and it definitely cost me some friends!

During the summers, I worked for Pioneer Hybrids as an agronomy researcher and analyst. I helped work on creating genetically-altered corn hybrids that could withstand pests and difficult weather conditions. I was on a team with some really great people who became wonderful friends. My boss, Steve Buss, loaned me the $900 to buy that old Toyota Tercel.

I ended up working there for about five years, and every summer starting in my sophomore year in college, it got harder. The mosquitoes in the north central United States are as big as cockroaches. Pollen hits your neck, and you start itching like crazy. Maybe I needed to find a different way to get to my goal. I thought to myself, this was brutal!

Then I heard that North Dakota and the Federal Department of Transportation had started a master's program in transportation in collaboration with North Dakota State University's college of agricultural economics. I knew I wanted to learn as much about agriculture as I could so that I could help feed African children, so I went and applied to join the program. NDSU offered me a full ride and an assistantship, and I was admitted with a dual major of agricultural economics and applied economics, with an emphasis in transportation. I took a role as a married couple's residence hall director, so I was basically being paid to go to school.

I was so pumped up that I immediately called my mother in Nigeria. "Mom, I just got accepted to North Dakota State," I told her. "I'm going to get my master's degree!"

"Oh, that's so exciting. What are you going to school for?" she asked. "Transportation!" I exclaimed.

You could have heard a pin drop!

In five or six seconds, she came back on the line. "Everybody goes to America to learn to be engineers and doctors," she lamented. "My son goes to America to learn how to be a truck driver!"

"No, mom!" I pleaded. "This is *transportation...* I'm going to help people in Africa learn how to move food from point A to point B. Don't worry, I'm not going to drive a truck or anything!"

We've enjoyed many good laughs about that conversation since then.

NUGGETS OF VIRTUE

I truly believe that we've all been put here on earth to make a difference. This model of determination towards a life of service was shown to us by the greatest philanthropist who ever lived, the greatest servant and minister who ever walked among us in this world. His name is Jesus Christ.

Jesus was a man of His word. He understood and accepted His responsibility to change the world, and the lessons He taught us during His short time on earth spur us on to follow in His footsteps.

As the apostle Paul exclaimed in Acts 20:24, "My life is worth nothing to me unless I use it for finishing the work assigned me by the Lord Jesus... the work of telling others the Good News about the wonderful grace of God!"

Jesus provides each of us with such an assignment. He instructs us to channel our energy towards something positive, to aim to make this world a better place by shining the light of the Lord into every corner. If we are obedient, we will directly see that our actions can impact and touch and change hearts and lives.

As I went through my college years, I was determined to fortify myself with skills and tools so that I could shine a bright light back towards my beloved home continent. I wanted to serve as a conduit to feed the needy of Nigeria, South Africa, and Mozambique, to help the children of Africa. To do this, I tried to learn how to grow nourishing food efficiently, and how best to move food products from places that had it in abundance to areas that desperately needed it.

I could never have known at the time that God had different plans for me. He would end up using my determination, my obedience to His will, in completely different and miraculously wonderful ways.

4: COMMITMENT

My wife and I, along with our first daughter Nike, moved into a tiny town home on the North Dakota State campus. While I was going to grad school there in Fargo, I was still working at Concordia, just a few miles to the east over the Minnesota-North Dakota border. Concordia allowed me to keep my shift as a campus policeman, and I worked 40 hours over the weekend from Friday to Monday—eight hours on and eight hours off.

It was tough. I'd be nodding off on Sunday mornings at church during the sermon, and those early Monday morning classes were brutal. I had to talk to my professor after class, because I was getting in trouble for falling asleep!

I had to apologize, and fully explain my situation. I was married, my wife and I just had our first baby, and I had to work 40 hours every weekend. I honestly didn't mean any disrespect.

But through it all I maintained an excellent grade point average. My advanced standing in the NDSU transportation program afforded me the opportunity to be a part of a professional organization called the Council of Logistics Management. It was a group full of CEO's and executives in the logistics business who met at different conferences around the country every year.

I was selected as one of the top 30 students in the country, and was invited to join them at a national conference in San Diego.

It was a week-long event, and I'd have to miss significant class time. I made arrangements with most of my professors. But when I told Dr. Won Koo that I wanted to go to this conference, he was unmoved.

"What's more important?" he asked me. "Econometrics, or some boondoggle in California?"

I was taken aback. I thought any professor would be excited to hear that one of their students had received a national honor. After all, I was one of a very few students nationwide selected to go to San Diego.

"If you attend this conference," Dr. Koo told me, "then you've made your bed. There's a test that week, and if you aren't present for that test, you will fail. Failure will bring your average for the course down to a D."

I went to the dean of our department and explained everything to him—and this was the word I used: I said that Dr. Koo was being a *jerk*!

"Don't worry, we'll talk to him," the dean assured me. It turned out that I was able to take the test after returning from my trip, so everything was okay.

I flew out to California. Every day at that convention, they'd profile one of the chosen students during the general session. They would show a picture of the student, and put together some bullet points of what he or she was doing back on campus. They featured me one day, and a group of people approached me afterwards.

Patrick, a Singaporean guy who would become one of my closest friends, asked me, "Are you interested in a job?"

"Sure, I want a job," I answered. "What's it to you?"

Patrick said he wanted to interview me and see a copy of my resume. He added that he was impressed by everything I had done during my college career. He said, "I'd like to fly you to Charlotte to meet my team."

Where is this Charlotte, I wondered? Even though I'd been in America for some time, I still was grappling with the sheer size of the United States. There were so many cities and states and places. I asked Patrick what the closest city to Charlotte was.

Atlanta, he told me, in the southeast corner of the country.

"Oh, that's gotta be warm," I said, rubbing my hands together. After years of living in North Dakota and Minnesota I was ready to move to any place that wasn't covered in snow most of the time!

In November 1995, Patrick flew me to the southeast to interview for a position in his company, which was called Metasys. I landed in Charlotte, and it was 75 degrees. When I'd left Fargo, it was 25 below zero with the windchill.

"This is what I'm talking about!" I said as I gladly took off my coat.

I went through the interview process, and they loved me. They made no secret of the fact that they wanted me to work there. I had a business way of thinking, and they saw I could be very technical too. I was so excited and pumped up, I wanted to work with these wonderful people in this great place where it was that warm in the middle of November.

They gave me an offer right in the middle of the interview! I thought, holy smokes, these guys don't play around! Where do I sign?

In all my enthusiasm, I caught myself. "I can't do anything right away," I told Patrick and his team. "I have to talk this over with Tracie."

But that was all just a minor delay and a formality. I got back to my hotel that night, and I called my wife from my room.

I said, "Honey, we've prayed about a lot of stuff together. But this one, we've just got to go ahead and move on. God's going to have to work the details later. Tracie, I'm telling you, it's 75 degrees down here! I'm an African dude, this is my kind of temperature!"

Tracie agreed. She'd had enough of windchills and temperatures with minus signs in front of them to last her a lifetime. So the family moved to Charlotte in March 1996, and we're still here. We haven't looked back. Since then, some of Tracie's family members have moved to North Carolina too, including her beloved mother.

There was still the matter of finishing my education. I was done with my course work, but I had to go back to Fargo to work on my thesis at NDSU. I was creating a least-cost shipping model for the transportation of a unique corn hybrid called waxy corn. Waxy corn is a type used primarily in Japan, a high-fructose hybrid that's high in carbohydrates and also has by-products that can be used in paint. I was trying to figure out the ideal location of a waxy corn processing center in the United States, and I was formulating effective shipping strategies. I ended up having to defend my thesis over the phone.

At Metasys, everything was going so well. I was driving the product group, and it was a real baptism by fire for the first few months. I wasn't a software developer, I was more of a business thinker. And this company was made up of great minds from top schools such as Duke, Wake Forest, and Cornell.

But I clicked with the guys on my team, I stepped up my game, and we all became as close as family. I was quickly promoted to a position where I became the product manager of the company's core flagship product, a software package called Metafreight.

I was responsible for helping conceptualize unique technology. I was working with a design team to build freight-management software that helped with appointment scheduling and freight organization. Metasys was the first supply-chain company to roll out a Web-based transportation software system, and at the time it was some very cool stuff. It seems like nothing nowadays in an age when everybody uses the Web for everything, but in 1996 we were one of the first companies in our industry to really harness the power of the Internet. We were working to bring together ocean shippers, transportation companies, trucking companies, warehousing companies so they could coordinate and efficiently move products from one place to another.

And to think, if I'd listened to Dr. Won Koo, I wouldn't have been a part of all of this! That "boondoggle" in California ended up changing the direction of my life.

As I look back, I'm amazed at how God ordered my life's series of events. Hindsight is always 20/20, but I didn't know at the time that this was all part of my boot camp to prepare me for what I'm doing today. For somebody who wanted to feed kids in Africa, I had no idea what I was doing at a software company! It's unbelievable how God orders your steps, then reveals the purpose later. Hindsight, foresight, sideways-sight... to Him, there's no difference.

Back in Nigeria, my father was getting ready to retire. He didn't really plan his retirement or put much money aside to secure the family's future.

The truth is that he drank most of his savings away.

He bought land, but never got around to building his retirement home. They were all living in the government quarters, in that two-bedroom house of my youth, but it was a government-owned home and the family would have to move out upon retirement. Where was my family going to live?

Most African kids are the "social security" for their parents. There's no government system which ensures that anyone will be taken care of in their old age. You support your family, that's all there is to it.

Even though my father and I didn't have the best relationship, even though there was still lingering resentment over the circumstances about my leaving Nigeria all those years ago, I felt like the greatest gift I could give was to honor my father. I liquidated my 401k and built them a house. I did it so that my father would not be shamed, and so that our family name would remain well-respected in the community.

My wife has been such a phenomenal supporter, and has given up so much to help my extended family. Agreeing to forfeit such a huge piece of our future was a major sacrifice for us.

But my father never had the opportunity to live in that house. His liver started to fail, and he was admitted to a hospital. His lungs stopped functioning properly, and his legs became swollen. Systems all across his body were shutting down, and he was finally diagnosed with advanced cirrhosis. Death was not a "how" or "maybe" for him anymore, it was a "when."

I was very concerned because I knew my father didn't have any kind of relationship with Christ. If he died, I thought, what would eternity be like for him?

So I called one of my sisters in Nigeria, and asked her, "Would you do me a favor? Would you go talk to our father for me? Would you ask dad this question... if he were to die today, does he know whether or not he will spend eternity in heaven with the Lord?"

My sister talked to our father, and she reported back to me. My dad was always a very strong guy, very resolute, and he never cried. But when my sister visited, he admitted that he was scared to die without having a relationship with Christ. He realized where he was going. He broke down in tears.

He knew what the score was.

On a hospital bed, my father prayed to ask Jesus Christ to come into his life. He begged for forgiveness for his sins. He asked the Lord to pardon him for all the damage and wreckage he had caused because of alcohol.

And through that process, my father and I found reconciliation. In my family, my mother and I always talked a lot, but I never really had the opportunity to talk about "man stuff." Everything I learned about being a man, I learned from myself or on the street. And in Africa, it's customary that sons are talked *at* instead of spoken *to*. That's the core difference between me and my father, it's a cultural one. My father and I had few heart-to-heart discussions when I was growing up, so we never got to really know each other. At the end, I thank God that we were able to talk a little bit more and make up for some lost time.

When I look over the entirety of my dad's life story, I know that even though he drank to excess and made bad choices, he was not a bad person. When I was very young, he was an awesome guy. Even while other people in our neighborhood were suffering in poverty, he broke his back to make sure that we had a good life. We didn't have everything—our water didn't run all the time, so we had to fetch water for all 13 people who were living in that small house. But he gave us the best he could.

Whenever he had some extra money, he would go to the grocery store and buy special meals for us, like eggs or sardines. Early in my youth, he took a lot of pride in his responsibilities as a father, and always tried his hardest to make us happy.

But my father progressively broke down under the pressure of family life. I really believe the reason why my dad spiraled out of control is because he simply grew up too fast. His father, my grandfather, was a police officer in Lagos who moved from place to place and had three wives. My dad was the oldest of their many children, and my grandfather passed away when my dad was a junior in high school. After that, he had to hurry up and finish school so he could lead and feed our family. On top of all that responsibility, he had to educate all his brothers and sisters so they could fend for themselves.

Lagos is very much like the New York City of Africa. My dad had to learn quickly how to think on his feet as a teenager, and even made some money as a boxer. He also had quite a local reputation as a playboy, so my mom's family didn't want her to marry this guy. "He's trouble," they warned her.

But she married him because she loved him. And I thank God that she did. I wouldn't be who I am today if those two wonderful people hadn't raised me.

I did learn some good traits from my father. He inspired a work ethic that I carried with me into my adulthood. He started with nothing, then graduated to become a gardener for the parks and recreation department for the state. He tended to the governor's residence, and he developed a knack for finding the right flowers and plants to make the property beautiful. The governor took notice, and sent him to Oxford, England, so he could take a course in landscaping. When he returned to Nigeria, he earned a series of promotions and became the head of landscaping operations for Lagos. He played a major role during his days to beautify our city.

However, his drinking increased and his life became different and strange. While I was going through puberty, the defining period in my life, my father was never there for me. He never came to my basketball games or took an interest in anything I was doing. The day I left for America, he didn't even give me a hug or shake my hand.

But I'll never forget one time during my sophomore year, a Parents' Day function. My father took the time to come to our school and take part. It was the first time he'd ever come to anything like that.

He was wearing a white African outfit. It was so clean and brilliant it looked like it was radiating light. I was so proud, pointing him out to my classmates as he entered the building. I had a big smile on my face, and I stuck my chest out. That day, I felt like I could fly.

"That's Mr. Ohonme," I told everybody who would listen. "He's my father."

One of the few pieces of wisdom my father passed along to me was this: "Emmanuel, never hang out with friends your age. You can't learn much from them. Always hang out with people who can teach you something."

I've carried that lesson with me. Most of my dad's friends were more than 10 years older than he was. In 2009, I turned 38, and realized that most of my friends at the time were in their late 40's and early 50's. These were people who had accomplished great things, and I learned from their experience. I studied their processes of success so I could emulate them, and I closely observed their missteps. I tried my hardest not to make the same errors.

My father made a lot of mistakes, and I learned much from them. Our family found out later that he had fathered a child outside of wedlock. A lot of choices that he made were wrongheaded and destructive, but my dad finally accepted Christ and invited Him into his heart.

Everyone around him could see the immediate difference in his life after that. For his last two weeks on earth, he was a totally different person.

My mother, who had been praying for him for years, was happiest of all. She taught me this valuable lesson: never give up praying for loved ones that are close to you but seemingly distant from the Lord. No matter how lost they become, God always has His eye on them. His plans and His purpose are as real and relevant for them as they are for us. God never gave up on my dad, and I know he's in heaven with the Lord now.

I look forward to the day when I'll see my biological father again. What a glorious day that's going to be... we have a lot of catching up to do.

I flew back to Nigeria to attend my father's funeral.

I hadn't been back to Lagos since the day I left for America. And it wasn't until I returned that I fully realized that our family, according to the world's standards, was horribly poor. Growing up, I never thought we lived in poverty. It never occurred to me.

When I walked into our house after all those years, I saw how dilapidated it really was. I had forgotten. Our bathroom was so dirty and broken that I couldn't even use it. I thought, my God, we actually lived like this! This was the home of my youth!

In Charlotte, I was living the American dream and had temporarily forgotten what my roots were.

Back in the country of my birth, I walked around the neighborhood. I saw children playing sports in Rowe Park, just like I had done when I was younger. There were kids playing basketball, running around chasing each other, kicking soccer balls. Many of them were barefoot, their feet caked with dirt and grime.

And right there, that's where the inspiration for Samaritan's Feet was ignited in my heart. We started Samaritan's Feet for those kids in that park.

People often think that our charity was birthed because of the fact that I received a pair of shoes from a missionary. That's the short and simple version of the story, and I'm glad for this opportunity to share the deeper and more complex version with you now.

Those shoes that Dave presented to me eventually wore out, and there was another missionary group that came along later with shoes... I didn't get any that time. I didn't receive another pair of tennis shoes until I was 16. It was my mother's bottomless, endless love that blessed me with my second pair; she saved up money to buy me a pair of brand new sneakers, so I could play in a basketball competition. They were Velcro and didn't have real laces, but I treated them like gold because they were a gift from my dear mother.

I remembered what it was like not to have shoes, and I knew what a pair of shoes meant to a poor child. As I walked around Rowe Park that day, seeing those children in their bare feet, my mind raced. What if we could bring shoes to these kids, and have basketball clinics, and also share the message of hope that Jesus Christ offers them?

But reality started hitting me. This was far too big of a challenge to handle. I had studied to feed African children, but that was all logistics and transportation and cerebral mind-work. Bringing shoes to African kids? Was I serious? Maybe it was the food I was eating; perhaps that was why I was having such crazy, insane thoughts! African people who go to America do so to chase a dream.

What was I thinking about coming back for?

I was having this internal struggle, but I knew I was being called to do something bigger than myself. That tug of war in my heart would take five years to work itself out.

When I came back from my trip to Nigeria in 1997, I was inspired to join the ministry. Most people are unaware that I'm Rev. Manny Ohonme, because I don't usually talk about it.

At my church, United Faith Assemblies of God in Charlotte, one of the pastors there became a director for the Berean University (now Global University) ministry program. My church signed up to be a satellite facility for Berean and offered a two-year, distance learning "Master's Commission" program. The program allowed entrants to go through quasi-seminary training without actually going through the main campus, which was located far away in Missouri.

I completed the two-year program because I knew that I was being called to something more. I wanted to be prepared.

I enrolled in an "on-the-job" training program for minister development. Most people that I know who went to seminary didn't do a quarter of the hands-on things that we did. But this was seminary on steroids! Rather than sitting around in a classroom, listening to theological lectures, this "on-the-job" pathway focused on more practical aspects. It was a very intense program where we learned every detail of ministry—how to minister to children, how to reach teenagers and adults, how to outreach to homeless people. We learned how to do street evangelism, minister to individuals who were having problems with drugs, and we were made ready for all sorts of different situations and contexts.

Berean provided practical ministry training for men and women who were called into God's work, without bogging them down with so much schoolwork that they lost the essence of what it is to be a minister. The school's philosophy was: time is short, time is running out, we need the next generation of leaders out on the street *now* so they can respond to real-world situations. It was not about sitting around in a classroom and having long professorial discussions about Jesus!

The director of our program, Pastor Cliff Maynard, was a phenomenal and practical teacher. I remember my first class. He said to us, "For the next two years, you'll have no weekends. Your weekends are *mine*."

Every Saturday, we would do different outreaches. We learned all sorts of practical things such as how to break bricks. We weren't doing construction projects or anything—we were getting up on stage in front of groups of teenagers and tearing phone books, smashing cement blocks, things of that nature. If you've ever heard of Todd Keene and the Power Team, that's the kind of performance we were giving. There would be 12 or 15 of us up on stage, we would do our power demonstrations, then tell them about Jesus. We had to grab the attention of those teenagers in some pretty unconventional ways!

One of my advantages was that when I grew up in Nigeria, I had the opportunity to evangelize on school buses. I remember how in my sophomore year, it was nothing for me to stand up in the school bus and start sharing my testimony. So I had some practice with evangelizing, but Pastor Maynard took it to a whole new level.

Each student was responsible for planning and organizing outreaches every weekend. We'd go to a location in downtown Charlotte, or out in rural North Carolina, and we'd have to figure out what tool we needed to use to reach the people. Our class would visit retirement homes, where most of the residents didn't have anybody to come and visit them. So we'd go and befriend these elderly folks, read the Bible and encourage them to stay strong and focused on loving the Lord.

We'd figure out which class member's strengths would be best suited to each project, and then we would go make it happen. Is this a sports kind of situation? Manny, put together a basketball clinic. My business skills also gave me project management ability, so I took on a real leadership role.

Charlotte, as a city, really does a good job tucking away and covering up the impoverished, so much so that our family had lived there for five years and we didn't even know there was a low-income Section 8 community across from our home. It was surrounded by trees, hidden from view.

We would go to some of the most run-down, low-income sections of the city to take the Good News. We'd cook hot dogs and play basketball with the kids. These experiences led to my wife and I taking on the responsibility of planning, planting, and building an inner-city children's ministry at Gladedale. The community really embraced us, and we saw so many lives touched.

Recently, I was at a shopping complex in Charlotte and these two twin brothers stopped me. I didn't know who these kids were at first. "You don't remember me?" one of them said. "Mr. Manny, Mr. Manny, don't you remember who we are?"

I was trying to picture them, to place them in my mind. Then I remembered those little chubby faces, and it struck me. Shakeem and Akeem. They were big boys now! "Did you use to live in Gladedale, by Old Providence?" I asked.

"Mr. Manny!" Akeem said. "We've been wondering where you've been! We still talk about you guys, how you used to play with us on Saturdays. You would come to church and feed us on Sunday mornings... you know, I'm going to college now!"

Going from that community to a college was a dream come true, Shakeem said—like flying from the earth to the moon.

We went into places where people were selling drugs. We took prayer walks through those areas, trying to clean the streets up. We knocked on doors and asked people if there was anything we could pray with them about. There were a couple times when we almost got shot walking through those blighted neighborhoods.

But God protected us. Nothing fazed our class, we'd go and minister to needy people. God always had His loving hands resting on us.

As part of our final requirement for graduation, we had to go homeless in Charlotte. That was one of the most unbelievable things I've ever done. We had to live a week without showering, without brushing our teeth, and we had to wear the same clothes every day.

We prepared, we prayed, and the Friday rolled around when we had to step out and enter the homeless world. We could only leave our houses with one dollar to our name. We had to beg for everything we needed, and we were required to completely blend in with the homeless community. We had to look like them, smell like them, talk like them, and act like them.

If I looked suspicious at all, the others would think I was a cop and freeze me out. I quickly learned the ropes of what it takes to survive on the street.

There's a system out there. I found out which fast food chains threw away their old burgers, and at what time of day. There was one gentleman every Saturday who came and fed hot dogs to all the street people.

This exercise presented a couple of interesting problems for me. Imagine being a software executive, trying to account for my homelessness with my coworkers and clients. I prayed none of my customers would see me out there like that. I thought, how would I ever explain?

Each of us had to stay on the street the first night. The second night we had to sleep in a shelter. There were two major shelters in Charlotte, the George Shinn Center and one off Tryon Street they called the "Dog Pound." I learned there were people in that city who were lawyers, office workers, bankers who had lost their homes and were staying in this shelter. Their pride was so destroyed that they couldn't look anybody in the eye. My heart was broken by this realization.

Those white-collar workers had the process figured out. They'd come in there to the "Dog Pound" after work in their suits, take them off, then roll up the pants and jackets under their mats—and sleep with their shoes on. Otherwise, others would steal their clothes and run away. I had to learn that process too, so what little of value I had with me didn't disappear.

There were people on the sidewalks who would cross to the other side of the street just so they wouldn't have to walk next to me. When I was begging for money, some would just drop it on the ground so they didn't have to touch me. I would pick up the money, then they would walk the other way.

After that week, I looked at this problem from a completely different perspective. This is why I make such an effort to treat homeless people with dignity and respect.

A group of us were inspired to start an outreach in 1998 where we'd feed homeless people. We'd cook them sausage, and fry up eggs, and make a big pot of grits. I didn't know grits smelled that nasty. I thought I'd have an appetite and taste for grits until I tried them once... I didn't know how people in this country could put something like that in their mouths. But I gladly cooked that stuff in my kitchen because my homeless friends in the South loved it. They'd put in butter, salt, pepper...

I just said, "God bless you, brother, none for me!"

There's a weekly breakfast in Charlotte, one that's still going on to this day, called Church On The Street. Every Sunday morning, a breakfast is served followed by a short church service. Up to 300 people come to those breakfasts, whether there's sun, snow, rain, or hail.

Going homeless was an important week-long exercise to experience how the poor in our city really lived, and I learned how to be able to minister to them on their level. We ended the week with a church service for the homeless, and our class members had a chance to minister to all these precious people that we had met on our short journeys. We were able to connect with them at a different depth and level of trust. Some of them were awakened to Christ by our involvement.

Some of the homeless I met that week and ministered to at Church on the Street are still homeless. They remember me when I go through the inner city; now they call me "shoe man." Many have made it off the street too, and I'm so happy for them.

I knew I was being called to do something big, but I was scared of the scope of what I was called to do. I didn't think anybody would believe me if I told people about my dream of putting shoes on the feet of children all over the world. Putting shoes on kids' feet? Who does anything like that? That's whacked, Manny. I thought my dream was far larger than I could handle, or even truly comprehend.

Honestly, I kept making excuses. I was mostly afraid of failing, because I had never failed in my entire life. For the first time, I wanted the proverbial cup of ministry to pass me by.

Tracie and I kept up our inner-city outreach. We preached at local prisons. I was serving on the board of an organization called Urban Restoration and helped them put together many of their summer programs. They had a sports program called Westside Olympics, in which I was very involved. I was always speaking at churches, sharing my testimony. Tracie and I led one of the biggest home groups at our church, the United Faith Assemblies of God (now called the Christlife Church). There were over 50 people coming to our home once and sometimes twice per month.

I kept myself busy. I was doing all these things, finding the time to serve. But these were all activities I could do while still holding on to my big house, my fancy car and my six-figure income. I was shelving the big dream and playing the comfort game. Throughout that process, learning to be a minister, I was going through the challenges of the call. A lot of people think that when God calls you to something, that it's easy to say Yes. Believe me, it's not.

I was scared of the gigantic responsibilities that came with Yes. How was I going to support my family? Not just my nuclear family at home, but also my extended family. All this was rushing through my mind. So I thought I'd go through the ministry program.

I'd do all the small things I knew how to do, and I'd still please God and fulfill my obligations to Him. I'd write checks, *anything* but pursuing this big dream. I could still meet God's criteria and stay in my comfortable bubble with my money and all my stuff. He wins, I win... everybody wins. Right?

But that was my plan, and then there was God's plan—and they turned out to be two very different entities. I'll put it in terms of an analogy that people from Charlotte will understand. Instead of going straight down I-85 and I-77, I took I-485, the loop around the city. I knew what I was called to do, to go straight down the middle and pursue my dream, but I took the *long* way around to get there. I graduated from Berean in late 1999, but Samaritan's Feet was still four years away.

At the threshold of Yes, there are responsibilities, obligations, and fears. You might have people telling you, "You can't do this, you can't follow this big dream. Don't you realize that you have to take care of your family?" All these voices, all these concerns, all these challenges. You're weighing these factors, while you know in the back of your mind that you're called to something that's bigger than yourself.

But you still try to avoid it.

Back when I was in high school, I'd avoid math as much as I could. I would take physics and chemistry if it meant that I didn't have to take a math class. My buddy would ask, "Is there something wrong with you? You're trying to escape this by trying to do something harder."

The path I had chosen by joining the ministry was demanding, but it didn't require any surrender or sacrifice. I was so comfortable. I was doing everything I wanted to do, surrounded by luxuries. I didn't want to give any of this up, I knew how missionaries lived! When Metasys was sold, there was the potential that it was going to go public during the craziness of the dot-com boom. Metasys ended up closing a multi-million dollar deal with Caliber Logistics, which at the time was one of the biggest logistics software deals ever. That led to the company being acquired in 1998.

But everything changed after that. Most of all, the spiritual climate changed. When we started out, Metasys was a company that always prayed together. Our team members were so close; we always supported each other and their families. We were interested in making millions of dollars, of course, but it was more than work to us. We believed that we were all part of a common dream at a unique point in history. We wanted to make sure that we were doing things in a way that honored God.

This way of thinking wasn't a priority for the new executives that came into the company after the acquisition. To be honest, some had a cold-blooded, cutthroat New York mentality. If anyone stood in the way of the company, this new crew would just take them out without any regard to the consequences. Their morality was questionable and certain practices infiltrated the operation—things we would have never done in the first three years of the company.

We had been a close-knit family, we always jokingly called ourselves the "Metasys Mafia." So it broke my heart when this lifestyle began rubbing off on the friends I'd been working with. Their commitment to God was being replaced by a selfish commitment to themselves. One of our original team members almost lost his wife and his beautiful children, because he succumbed to temptation and cheated. When I saw this, I knew I had to get out of this poisoned environment. In my heart I knew it was time to move on.

NUGGETS OF VIRTUE

Satan always looks appealing, if only for a few minutes; but the repercussions destroy for an eternity. The adversary of God prowls around looking for someone to destroy, and each of us must be vigilant. Satan is searching for every small crack during every moment of vulnerability. He will do anything to seize your destiny from you.

But when we enter treacherous territory, when temptation is all around us, God is with us also. He is constantly by our side to give us strength against the enemy, should we choose to rely on His power.

Our Savior, during His short time on this earth, was lured by temptation. Right after His baptism, as described in the fourth chapters of both Matthew and Luke, the Holy Spirit led Jesus into the wilderness, where Satan tested Him three times.

Satan dared Jesus to perform a cheap miracle, to put Himself in unnecessary danger to test His Father's protection, and to trade His heavenly kingdom for an earthly one. Using all the strength His temporary flesh could muster, Jesus refused. He knew that He was on a path that led to His destiny, and did not waver from His commitment to stay on the course.

God provides a way of escape from every temptation: commitment. If you are on a righteous path, the enemy will always be hovering by your side, attempting to lure you astray. Temptation is a constant companion.

Never let down your guard. Keep your eyes focused on the prize. Keep moving forward, and keep God in your heart.

5: SURRENDER

In 1998, I left Metasys, the company that brought me to Charlotte. I hooked up with a buddy of mine in New York who ran a company called Syntra Technologies. Pano Anthos was the CEO there. They were in the global commerce management space, developing software that allows major international shippers to manage trade regulations aspects of their global commerce. They were introducing a new line of transportation software, and they wanted me to help drive a marketing strategy for that product.

One of my sisters had moved to New York and my wife's uncle lived there as well. I thought maybe this could be a way to get closer to family in that area. Syntra gave me an offer right away, and said they would pay for weekly flights between Charlotte and New York so I could commute.

The travel was hard on my family, but Tracie realized she couldn't move the family to New York.

So I fulfilled my contractual obligation for a year, and it was a tough 12-plus months. Being away for so long was hard on us all. Our third daughter, Yemi, was born during that time, and I didn't get to fully participate in that process.

In 2000, one of the guys who worked for me at my old firm called me up. Travis Parson, a buddy of ours, was starting a new company in

Charlotte called Elogex. "Travis wants to talk to you about coming to help. This could be an incredible opportunity. There's plenty of upside."

At first, I was hesitant. There is always a huge amount of risk with a startup. But this was happening in Charlotte, and I'd be able to be back with my family seven days a week. I had a feeling I should look into it.

Travis and I hit it off instantly, and I accepted the position. I led the marketing and product management group, and we unleashed an appointment scheduling solution for large grocery retailers that was the first of its kind. We revolutionized the transportation software business, helping the likes of Kroger and Safeway of the world to become more efficient, coordinating shipments for thousands of items to affiliated stores across the country. We had many of the major grocery chains from coast to coast as our customers, and we helped save them millions of hours and dollars. Our software helped pave the way for the mega-supermarkets of the 21st Century.

Our company had such a unique product that we had access to a huge initial round of funding.

In late 2002, we went through a mammoth fund-raising cycle. In 2003, when the venture capital partners committed the funds to us, they said, "You're a bunch of 30-year-old guys, trying to manage almost $30 million. You all need some adult supervision!"

So they brought in another layer of executive management. One of them, John Rollins (who went by "J") was brought in as a contractor by the incoming chief operating officer, and J's job was to oversee sales and marketing. So I was reporting directly to him in this new hierarchy.

Our little company was undergoing much explosive growth, but it was getting hard for me to stay. I knew when that new layer of management came in that I wasn't supposed to be there. I was hanging on.

Elogex was looking at acquiring or merging with a procurement and order management software company in Texas called OMI International. So J and I were sent down to Dallas to check things out. In February 2003, we flew into the airport one late afternoon. Our meeting at OMI wasn't until the next morning, so J had an idea for an evening's entertainment.

"Do you want to go see a basketball game?" he asked me. "The Dallas Mavericks are in town, they're playing the New Jersey Nets tonight. Let's try to get tickets."

We went down to the arena that evening and paid a scalper for seats. It was a very important game, and it wasn't because J and I saw Dirk Nowitski and a young Steve Nash lead the Mavericks to a big late-season victory. For me, it was a defining night. In fact, J kept his ticket and presented it to me as a gift five years later, to remind me of that moment.

That evening, I was inspired to share my vision with J as we waited for the game to begin. I just started running my mouth. I excitedly told him about my big dream, of that day in Nigeria when I went back for my father's funeral and the inspiration I received from seeing those kids in Rowe Park.

I told him about an organization that existed only in my mind. It was called "Samaritan's Feet," and we would travel around the world and give shoes to poor kids so they could play sports.

J sat there and listened to me for half an hour. Finally, he stopped me. "Why are you still here, Manny?" he asked.

"Why am I..." I replied, stunned. "What do you mean?"

"Manny," J said, "if you have this much passion for this, about putting shoes on kids' feet, what are you doing working for Elogex?"

I started backtracking, telling him how my three children needed to eat. I was changing the subject as fast as I could. This guy (who was my boss, no less) was confronting me about this gigantic dream I'd been trying to find every reason to say No to for so many years! I'd given God every excuse in the world, and here was this executive laying it all out there in such simple terms.

We watched the game, went back to the hotel, and in the morning we had our meeting. It went well, but we ended up not doing anything further with that company.

At the time, Tracie and I knew in our hearts we were being called to something huge, but we didn't know how to take that step of faith. God couldn't get through to me directly, and He couldn't get me to say "Yes" right away.

But He got to me through my wife.

Right around the same time that J and I went to Texas, Tracie attended a women's conference in Greensboro, North Carolina. She traveled to the venue with five ladies, two of whom she was meeting for the first time. The event was led by Joyce Meyer, a popular and influential Christian speaker who inspires ladies to be godly women and do significant things in the world. There were around 10,000 people in attendance.

After the first day of the conference, as they were returning to the hotel, a lady that Tracie had just met pulled her aside. "Is it okay if I talk to you?"

The lady told Tracie, "God has called you and your husband towards a big dream, but you guys keep putting God in a box. You've been giving Him every excuse, but the time for excuses is over. The two of you need to repent and say Yes, and be obedient to what God wants you to do."

My wife's jaw dropped. She couldn't believe what she was hearing. This lady could discern the struggles we were going through, as we tried to find a foothold on the path towards our destiny of service.

Then that woman did something, and we didn't realize until a year after we started the ministry how symbolic it was. She had a bottle of Deer Park water with her. When she was talking to Tracie, she said, "If it's okay with you, would you allow me to wash your feet?"

And she proceeded to wash Tracie's feet, using the process described in John 13.

"God's going to use your uniqueness as a couple," that woman told my wife. "Manny is black and you are white, and since you are unique, it will open many doors. The Lord is going to raise an army of young people around the world who you will be able to touch."

God definitely spoke through this woman. She told Tracie of a vision she had, of a convoy of trucks with resources being mobilized to reach the poor around the world. (And that vision was made real six years later, when Kmart gave Samaritan's Feet a million pairs of shoes... which were delivered using a convoy of over 200 truckloads.)

Little by little, God's big picture was revealed. Tracie came home after the meeting and she wrote down what had been said to her. Later on, after the children had gone to bed, she confronted and challenged me.

"Honey, we've been disobedient," she said. "What is it going to take for us to honor what God's calling us to do?"

I was taken aback. As we continued talking, we formed a short-term plan. I didn't need any confirmation of my dream, I had plenty of that. But I wanted to make absolutely sure.

"Tracie, we have to be certain this is really God talking," I said. "We have to go get some space, pray about this, and seek God's direction."

That's when we went on a retreat, which is something we always do whenever we are faced with a major life decision. Tracie and I found someone to watch the kids and we drove down to Charleston, South Carolina.

We just wanted to seek counsel without any distractions. That weekend, we tried to envision a world without steady corporate income, one in which we were completely sold out to a life of service. We prayed to find some much-needed inner peace.

On Saturday, March 28, 2003, in the afternoon, we were sitting in our hotel room overlooking the water. We were just talking. It was nothing spiritual, just a nuts-and-bolts kind of conversation like we always have. Tracie repeated her challenge.

"What is it going to take for you to go do this?"

I wasn't ready yet to make that decision, but I got the ball rolling by doing some quick calculations. Between our savings and the cash we had on hand, I figured that if we had another six months' worth of living expenses, we'd be able to survive without a paycheck for at least a year.

"I think we should be fine if we do this," I said.

We enjoyed a lovely dinner and the next morning went to church before we drove home.

On Monday morning, I went in to work at Elogex as usual. It started out as an ordinary day. I took my conference calls like I always did, I talked to our alliance partners, I chatted with our sales guys. Right before 12 o'clock, I was about to go to lunch so I poked my head into J's office. "Hey, want to go grab a bite?" I asked.

J looked very serious. "Manny, come in here," he said. "I want to talk to you."

"What's going on?"

He shut the door behind us. This he had never done before. "I want to talk to you about something very important," J said.

"Someone else is coming in who's going to take over your job," J told me, flat out. "Our chief operating officer was supposed to have this conversation with you later today, but I felt that it was better if I talked to you about it."

I was shocked. I was number four or five in the chain of command, and had helped build the company up from nothing to over 100 employees. And the carpet was about to be pulled out from under me. Because we were originally a startup, I didn't sign an employment contract that guaranteed me a severance package.

Within that founding group, we all trusted each other. Nobody had bothered to sign anything when the venture capital money started flowing, or when the new managers had been brought in. I knew I'd learned a valuable business lesson, but it was too late to put it into practice.

"This isn't happening," I thought in complete disbelief. "This just can't be happening."

J grabbed my shoulders and squared me up. "Remember that conversation we had in Dallas a few weeks ago?" he reminded me. "Remember when you were sharing your vision for this organization called Samaritan's Feet?"

"Yes, I do," I managed to say.

"What if I can help you get it started?"

"What are you talking about, J?"

I was getting mad now. In fact, I was furious. I was about to lose my job, everything I'd ever worked for. I was losing my work, and the pride of a man just sprung up inside me. I was too blinded by anger at that moment to see the big picture God was painting.

But J stuck with me and remained calm. "Manny, I think I can help get you some resources. I know you can probably stay here and work in services or something, but you don't want to do that. You don't want to travel like those people do. That night at that basketball game, I remember the fire in your face, and the passion in your voice. I think I can help you. Our COO and I talked, and he's open to giving you a severance package."

I recalled the conversation I'd had two days previous with my wife in Charleston. The severance promised would be equal to that six months' worth of living expenses we'd discussed.

This was as if God was telling me, "You asked for it!"

I left that office, I didn't even grab my laptop, I just headed home. I called my wife on my cell phone, and she could tell immediately that something was wrong. "Honey, what's the matter?" she asked me.

"I think my days at Elogex are over," I said.

"What are you talking about?"

"They want to bring in someone else to take over my job," I replied, starting to cry. "They're letting me go."

"Just come home," she told me with care and concern. "I'm here."

I drove back to my house and hung out with my wife, crying like a baby in her arms. Tracie encouraged me with words I will never forget.

"To him whom God calls, He always equips," she said. "I know you're scared, and you don't know how this is going to play out. But God's going to make a way."

If I wasn't a Christian, I would have called this day "Dark Monday." For the first time in my life, somebody was telling me they were taking my job.

I'd always been in the driver's seat. But what could have easily been the worst day in my life became the brightest. I told our former COO recently that he was one of the greatest instruments God used through this entire process. Because if he hadn't done what he had, I wouldn't be where I am today.

People glibly say they trust God. It's such a common concept that it's printed on every American dollar bill and coin. If you have a steady job, and every two weeks money is showing up in your bank account by direct deposit, that's a concept anybody can trust!

But most individuals haven't really had to *trust God* for every dime they make. Not knowing where your paycheck is going to come from requires a deeper level of trust. If you don't know how you're going to feed your children or keep the roof over your head, you have to trust God 100 percent.

Tracie and I stepped out of the doorway into this new challenge, not knowing where the other foot was going to land. I could have gone and secured another six-figure income, but I knew God had something bigger in store.

We knew we were called to perform a simple vision: to wash the feet of the poor and put shoes on the feet of kids, and to use sports to share a message of hope.

NUGGETS OF VIRTUE

A journey of obedience begins with complete surrender, once you realize that you are no longer the one in control and God is in the driver's seat. He created us with a specific void that only He can fill.

Some people try to fill this gap with careers, others attempt to pour drugs, alcohol, or sex into the vacuum. The world is desperately trying to fill that void with these earthly distractions. But sooner or later we have to realize that none of those things can properly fill the emptiness inside us. After we say Yes, nothing else can feel as satisfying, nothing else can ever fill the void... except God.

My journey of surrender started when I finally said "Yes" and launched Samaritan's Feet.

With certain life goals you set out for yourself, you might wonder if it's really your goal or God's. Many human beings (especially Type A personalities) are wired with the drive to make things happen. You might know what you want to accomplish, and go for it with everything you have. Oftentimes, you can spiritualize some of those things and say, "Yes, this is God driving me." But you yourself might be both the vehicle and the driver; sometimes you're just inviting God to ride along in the back seat.

Surrendering to His will is a journey—a purification process in which God has to empty you of yourself. We have so much baggage that we accumulate in life. Even though we can say "Yes, we surrender, Yes, we want to do everything You tell us to," that might not be enough. For example, there was once this guy named Manny in North Carolina who wanted to stay in his comfortable world and do local, small projects to help God, but that was really Plan B.

The Lord doesn't like Plan B, He only has one plan! That is the one He's ordained, and each one of us plays a role in its fulfillment. I had to go through a process of humility and humbling to get aligned with what God had in store for me.

For lack of a better phrase, the Lord had to remove Manny from Manny.

Some people, when God calls them, are willing and able to say "Yes" right away. But most are knuckleheads like me, who may have the best of intentions, but hold out as long as they can. I was hanging onto the "flesh side." I kept on justifying everything I was doing. I had children that needed to eat and be educated; I had a wife that loved to shop sometimes, and we all enjoyed going on vacation. My job had become a false idol.

I was rationalizing my stubbornness to remain in my comfort zone. I was telling myself that I was still being used by God where I was—even though in the back of my mind, I knew I was divinely called to do something on a much larger scale. God had to take all of this away from me, to remove those luxuries, in order for me to pursue the big dream.

Of course, I was very comfortable in my world. I loved making a six-figure income. I loved being able to go to Disney World two or three times a year, and I loved bringing my family along with me on business trips. I loved our big home and the flexibility that having money gave us. But all of this was robbing me of the ultimate goal, the enormous call that God had for me. My daily life was an obstacle to what the Lord wanted to accomplish through me: to make me His pipeline to impact millions on this planet. I don't know what size shoes God wears, but I felt Him kick me right in my backside. He jolted me out of my safe environment!

The Lord had to take away who I was. The bottom line is that Manny had to be crucified for God to come alive in me.

6: PERSEVERANCE

People have commented, "Manny, you guys are out there all over the world." But I reply, "You should have dropped by at the beginning!"

When we started Samaritan's Feet in 2003, Tracie and I were the team that raised the shoes, trained the volunteers, booked the travel, and coordinated the accommodations. We warehoused the shoes and packed them ourselves. Most of the things that needed to be accomplished were done by us, until we reached the point where we were big enough to attract the kind of staff that could take some of the responsibilities off our plate. Things have changed a lot over the years.

The greatest tool that prepared me was the ability to help run an organization. Samaritan's Feet is much more than just a regular company. There are so many aspects to it, things that I didn't have to think about when I was in the software business. Suddenly I was the chief financial officer, and at some point I became the chief development officer, the chief logistics officer, and also the one who swept the floors at night. As I tell people, I went from the "Boardroom" to the "Warehouse" all in one day.

We held meetings at a restaurant called Le Peep, which I used to call my "worldwide headquarters." They had a little room in the back where the doors closed. One of the first gifts Samaritan's Feet ever received was from Travis Parson, the founder of Elogex, who gave us an LCD projector so I could share presentations with local businesspeople about our vision. Thankfully, some gave donations.

We knew that we wanted to give shoes to millions of children. I felt that the vision God gives us has to be God-sized, so I told the members of our board that we were going to reach 10 million children. They basically just fell off their chairs!

They cautioned, "What!? Manny, you don't even know the shoe business!"

"I don't," I replied, smiling. "But I know the One who does. If you have a God-inspired vision to do something this big, you have to know that you can't accomplish it by yourself."

I found out later, after doing some research, that there are over 300 million children in the world who need shoes. But then we calculated that there are actually *3.1 billion*. That's over half of the population of the world. World Vision estimates that 3.1 billion people live on $1 and $2 a day. If the average cost of a pair of shoes is $10, there's no way they can afford them.

But we couldn't say we were going to raise 3.1 billion pairs of shoes, because no one would ever believe we could achieve that goal. We picked 300 million as a believable, obtainable number, and we targeted our goal toward children. They were the most vulnerable and desperate for the kind of help we wanted to provide.

We boiled it down to a series of numbers that would lead and guide us. Our objective was to put 10 million pairs of shoes on the feet of 10 million children in 10 years. And we began to strive towards that goal.

Keith White, who runs a sports ministry, was one of the first individuals I spoke to concerning what God was laying on my heart, back when I was still in the corporate world. I shared with him my big dream of using shoes and sports as vehicles to reach children and inspire hope.

"So what will you guys be doing in this ministry?" Keith asked.

"I want to take people to go and wash the feet of the poor, and teach sports and basketball, and do 3-on-3 tournaments, events such as that," I told him.

When I finally surrendered to the Lord and said "Yes" and started Samaritan's Feet, Keith came back to visit me.

"Are you ready for this?" he asked.

"Buddy, I don't know if I am," I told him. "But I think God's thrown me into this world, and now I have to live in it."

Keith was very helpful and said he'd made some phone calls to help me get things rolling. He really gave a shot in the arm to Samaritan's Feet by establishing connections and strategic partnerships in Charlotte. One day, he phoned me.

"Are you ready to go to South Africa?"

I asked Keith if he was crazy. South Africa?!

Keith told me he had already talked to his missions partner on the ground in Cape Town and they loved the concept of giving kids shoes and washing their feet.

"They're ready for you," he said.

I certainly wasn't! All of this was coming at me a little too quickly!

So I found myself partnering with a school in Charlotte called Hornets Nest Elementary School. Hornets Nest hosted our first-ever shoe drive, and they raised over 800 pairs of shoes for our new charity. Terroll Joiner, a former co-worker at Elogex, was instrumental in coordinating this effort, as his son attended school there.

When we first started Samaritan's Feet, our house was the "warehouse." Our garage was packed with shoes, our sun room and kitchen area were full, our living room was piled ceiling high. And let me tell you, our place stunk! At that time we were not just collecting new shoes, we were also taking in those that were "gently used." Tracie and I quickly came to the realization that people have many different interpretations about what "gently used" means!

We had to clean those dirty, muck-covered shoes, and we washed some of them two or three times. I was turning my wife's laundry room into a commercial laundry facility. But then all those heavy loads ended up breaking our washing machine. Tracie went through a lot of tests and trials during those early days. Poor girl! She was a committed soldier.

Over time, as we went through our first few shoe distributions, we realized the implications of giving out used shoes. Imagine being in South Africa or Nigeria, and 500 kids to whom you've promised shoes are coming through the door. On the right, there's a child whose feet you're washing, and you're putting a clean white pair of socks and a brand new pair of shoes on their feet. But to the left of that child is another kid from the same neighborhood. You've washed their feet, loved on them. And now you have the shoes laid out for them, and they've got this North Carolina clay stained on them. Those shoes may have been washed and cleaned, but that clay isn't coming out any time soon!

The two children have both been poor all their lives. Why did one kid get a brand new pair of shoes, and why did the other get shoes that someone had worn while mowing their lawn? It doesn't take much to know that something is wrong with this picture.

I know that when my children get new shoes, the excitement is unbelievable. Most of those kids in impoverished communities have never really experienced or understood "new" before.

It comes down to this: when God blesses us, He always gives us His best. God never gives us hand-me-downs or leftovers. I believe those kids are the children of the world and children of God, so they deserve our best. The Samaritan's Feet board passed a resolution that from that day on, we'd only accept new shoes. If we were going to give children anything in the name of our Lord, we had to give the absolute finest we had.

Now that we're shipping tens of thousands of new shoes in containers around the world, it's mind-boggling to see what God has done in just these few years. Tracie and I regularly reflect on those early days... now we have over a million pairs of shoes in warehouses across the country. "We've come a long way, Emmanuel," she says, laughing.

It's light years away from broken washing machines and smelly sneakers! In the beginning, if the shoes didn't have laces on them we'd have to go buy them at the store. We dried those used shoes and packed them in large canvas bags.

When it was time to take off on our first trip we loaded them all on a truck to bring to the airport. The volunteer team met up with us and we checked all the shoes as baggage, and we boarded the plane and were off to South Africa.

While all this was going on, the major paper in town, the *Charlotte Observer*, wrote an article about us and what we were trying to do. That story was a catalyst to propel Samaritan's Feet forward, it was a crucial milestone in our development. The lady who wrote the feature, Jeri Krentz, titled that article "Miracle of the Shoes."

I remember the picture in the *Observer* of our garage filled with shoes, with our family sitting on the stacks of boxes. That was our global worldwide warehouse and shipping center! Every great thing has a humble beginning, I guess. I remember that the photographer asked Tracie, "How in the world did you let him talk you into this?"

"I'm still trying to figure that out," my wife replied.

A friend of mine, Robert Walker, published a magazine called *Sports Spectrum,* which is written and read by many Christian athletes. After we returned from South Africa, Robert heard the reports of our trip and was fired up.

He told me, "Manny, I'd like to profile you in our magazine." So I went to his office for an interview.

After our session was over, he asked me, "Manny, have you ever thought about having your own brand of shoes made?"

"Rob, I was just an African boy who had no shoes," I replied. "You're talking about us having our own line of shoes?! Even I didn't dream *that* big! But if God can use a Samaritan's Feet shoe as a conduit, I will be all over that, brother."

"Let me tell you why I think this would be so cool," he continued. "I know a guy who's a Christian businessman who runs a manufacturing plant operation in China. Many of the people working at his plant are not believers. Imagine if we could make a shoe with the verse John 3:16 right there on the tongue of the shoe. Every time one of those workers at the manufacturing plant processes a pair, they'd be getting the word of God in them. This is a mission with a whole different dynamic."

I exploded with excitement. "Wow, that would be *huge!*"

I immediately envisioned a shoe that would feature an emblem to remind people why we do what we do. "If we could have an imprint of the cross in the sole of the shoe, everywhere the wearer steps, they'd leave the symbol of the cross behind."

"Manny, now you're getting me really excited," Rob said. "I've got to dial up that friend of mine."

So we set up a conference call for the next week.

On February 13, 2004, a Friday morning, I was headed to a meeting with a pastor in Charlotte to share my vision. I was going to figure out how we could collaborate and partner with some of his church groups. The night before, Charlotte had one of the worst frost snaps that had ever come through the city, as a clipper system unexpectedly passed through the area. In the southeast United States, whenever there's any kind of snow or ice, things shut down.

The country club near where I live had forgotten to turn the sprinkler system off. So when I left my home in the morning, I got on the main road which was caked with a thick layer of ice. I drove a Lincoln Navigator at the time, so I really didn't think anything of it. When I lived in North Dakota, I'd learned to drive a Toyota Tercel through a blizzard, so I knew I could get around in this kind of weather— especially in a 4x4 Navigator.

I wasn't on the road for more than a minute when it felt like somebody literally took the steering wheel from out of my hands. My SUV lost complete control, and careened right through the median.

There are streetlights between the lanes on the median, and to this day I do not know how my vehicle navigated between those streetlights. On the opposite lane, going the wrong way, I was suddenly in the path of an oncoming car. In a split-second, I was in a head-on collision with a Chevrolet Camaro.

BOOM! That was the first thing I heard.

BAM! Then a Ford F-150 hit me. **BANG!** And another car. **BANG! BANG!** Four or five vehicles in a row; loud crashes one after another.

The airbag inflated, opening up in front of me. All I could see was that airbag, and I was covered in a sea of white powder. I remember thinking if this is what heaven looks like, it didn't look good at all.

I was scared out of my wits. I didn't know if I was dead or alive.

The SUV came to a complete stop. I saw out of my window that the Camaro had been turned around, facing the other way, and I could see that a lady's head was resting on the steering wheel.

She wasn't moving. I started to freak out. I've never been that scared in my life.

Dear God. Had I just killed somebody?

This woman couldn't die on my watch. I started to pray to the Lord, this lady cannot die. God, God, Jesus, no...

My Navigator was completely totaled. I saw pieces of the Camaro all over the road. The other vehicles were collapsed together in a giant heap of jagged metal. People were emerging from their broken cars, stumbling and slipping on the ice.

Three minutes later, I heard the sirens of the fire engines coming closer. The emergency vehicles couldn't even get to the accident site. The drivers became stuck in the ice, so they had to find a way to maneuver around and get to us. The emergency medical technicians started doing triage. Two police officers began going through the wreckage. They didn't even come over to my SUV, and I was wondering why.

Then I saw the woman lift her head, just slightly. I saw her cough. I've never seen a cough look so good in all my life. The idea that I may have killed another human being was terrifying. But to see her head rise up, all I could think was, Lord, oh thank You, thank You!

The medical team stabilized her neck, took her vital signs, and placed her on a stretcher. I later found out that they took her to the hospital just to check everything out, and I learned she suffered no major injuries—just a large bruise on her shoulder from the impact of the seat belt. Other people in the pileup had some cuts and scrapes, but everybody survived the crash.

After they went through all the vehicles and stabilized everyone, the EMT's finally came over to my SUV. The police looked in the window from a distance and thought there was nobody inside. They assumed that whoever was driving this Navigator had to be dead.

But it couldn't have been a projectile-type situation, because the windshield was still intact. Surely nobody could have come out of this vehicle alive, so they checked it out.

One of the officers yelled, "Who's the driver of this vehicle?"

I motioned. I was tucked behind the fire truck barrier.

"Somebody's been praying for you," one of the responders said to me.

I replied, "Buddy, I hope they don't stop."

I was told later in the day that the city council had been warning people in the community to turn off their sprinklers whenever there was a forecast for freezing temperatures. Apparently some people didn't get the message. I just thanked God that nobody was seriously hurt, and I wanted to move on with my life.

All this happened on the day I was supposed to have that conference call with Rob and his friend, the manufacturer in China, who were going to help us make a branded shoe for Samaritan's Feet. I ended up missing the original conference call, while I was dealing with the paperwork after my wreck.

Rob called me and asked what happened.

"I think the enemy tried to take me out today," I told him. "I was involved in a car accident, but by the grace of God, I'm still alive. Don't cancel the call, let's make sure we get this done. I'm not going to let anything rob me of this opportunity."

We rescheduled for later that day, and I told that manufacturer the whole story about what we were trying to do in the world. He was so moved that he committed to fund the prototype of our Samaritan's Feet shoe. And that laid the foundation for the full-scale production of our branded shoes several years later. Nowadays, they make up about two percent of our worldwide inventory.

Instead of a swoosh or stripes, our shoes have our barefoot "SF" logo on the side! But due to sensitivity to other religions in countries where we work, the cross cut into the bottom of the sole was dropped from the final design. But wherever the wearer walks, those shoes still leave an imprinted reminder of Jesus' ultimate sacrifice in their minds.

"I want to be a part of your vision, Manny," the manufacturer said. "To put 10 million pairs of shoes on the feet of 10 million kids in 10 years. I want to be part of something that huge."

But none of this happened right away. There was still a long way to go, many more struggles and obstacles lay ahead of us.

When I was on the retreat in Charleston with Tracie, right before I said "Yes," I asked God for six months' worth of income to help cushion our family's finances. I didn't ask Him directly, this was all just conversation. But God was listening, and answered me by taking my job days later and using J to give me a severance package. God works quickly!

Tracie and I had given up my 401k when my father retired, but we had some savings left. I was going to collect unemployment, so I realistically figured that we had enough to live comfortably for the following year... maybe even a year and a half. If God chose to save all those persecuted kids in Darfur and forgot about me for a little while, our family would be okay.

That's what I thought, at least.

The next morning, less than 24 hours after my accident, my wife was driving our second daughter to a birthday party just outside of Charlotte. She turned onto Highway 200, while an old lady was approaching the same road. She didn't see my wife as she turned onto the road from the left through this major intersection.

The woman T-boned my wife's car.

I remember Tracie calling, asking me to come pick her up. "I've been in an accident," she said. I remember thinking initially that it was some kind of sick humor or something—after all, I'd just been in a bad car wreck the morning before.

But when Tracie started crying, I knew that it was true. "Please come get me," she pleaded.

Because my Navigator had been totaled the day before, I had to call in a favor to a friend. "What's wrong?" he asked when I phoned.

"Jin Leong," I said. "Tracie's been in a car accident outside of town. I need to borrow your car."

"You guys don't have very good driving records," he said, only halfway joking. "I'm on my way to come and pick you up, brother."

We drove to the scene outside Charlotte. Just as with my accident the day before, my wife, thankfully, didn't have a scratch on her. My daughter wasn't injured at all either. But our car was completely ruined. I thought that when I said "Yes" to God, everything would be perfect after that moment. I believed I had signed up for divine protection, that "Yes" membership had its privileges. I didn't bargain for this!

I was unaware that this was all part of my humbling process. I've always been the strong one, always in charge of everything. But I had to take a back seat—God had to be in control.

A truck came and towed our car away. In just 24 hours, we had become carless! Things were very difficult for our family for a while after that, trying to carpool or borrow friends' cars to get where we needed to go. It seemed we were always asking for rides.

About a month later, a friend of mine who owns a business in Charlotte invited my wife and me to his home. His name is Eric, and after his wife cooked a phenomenal meal for us he called me outside to talk. "Manny," he said, "I need to ask you for your forgiveness."

"Forgiveness?" I asked. "Eric, what on earth do you mean?"

"The Lord told me about a month ago that I was supposed to give you a vehicle," he explained. "But I didn't want to. My wife tried to convince me to do it, but I wouldn't call you. I kept putting it off. And I've realized over the last couple of weeks that I've been disobedient to God, that I've missed my blessing. If it's okay with you, I'd like to give your family my van."

I leapt up into the air and hugged Eric. "Buddy! We haven't had a car of our own for a month, thank you very much!"

Eric gifted us with a beautiful van that our family could use.

God replaced our totaled vehicles over time, but while this was all happening, our financial resources were being depleted. A couple of months afterwards, our daughter Nike woke up in the middle of the night screaming in pain. Her appendix was rupturing.

I no longer had the fancy corporate health insurance that our family had enjoyed for so long. I remember taking Nike to the emergency room very late that night in our new van. As soon as we reached the hospital, they performed tests, and then the doctors rushed her to the operating room. A nurse told me that if we'd arrived just five minutes later, our daughter could have suffered some serious complications. They had to remove her appendix right away.

They were very healthcare-friendly at that hospital—in other words, if you didn't have proof of insurance, you had to hand over a chunk of cash or cut a check before the doctors would even lift a finger. I remember how it felt to write that check, I could feel that severance money just disappearing and disappearing...

As we went through this process of surrender, every time some new adversity would strike, Tracie tried to remain calm. But she would become so upset in her private moments.

"Why is all this happening?" my wife would cry out when she prayed.

I kept telling Tracie, "God's just giving me real-world preaching material. We have to keep persevering."

Six weeks after Nike's surgery, my youngest daughter Yemi was playing outside in front of our house. She fell and broke her elbow. We had to return to the emergency room, pay out of pocket again, and go back through that entire cash-and-carry medical process.

I prayed to the Lord as I put the pen-strokes on another check. How low can I go, God? What is going on here?

The money that I thought was going to last our family for over a year was gone in four months. From a human economic perspective, when you say "Yes" to the God of the universe, you might think that everything will be alright. But one of my favorite scriptures is found in Psalm 51:17: "A sacrifice to God is a broken spirit; a broken and contrite heart He will not despise."

The Lord had to break my spirit so that I would become fully dependent on Him.

The straw that broke the camel's back came soon after Yemi's arm was put in a cast. Tracie went to a grocery store to purchase some supplies for our home. The total of the bill was $14.20, but all she had in her pocket was 12 dollars and some change. She couldn't come up with two dollars.

My wife called me, in tears. "Manny, what are you doing to me?" Tracie said over and over.

"I don't want these real-world stories anymore," she said. "We have to make money somehow. This is putting our family in serious danger."

That was my lowest point. God had completely broken me.

I dropped to my knees and prayed, "Lord, I need You now more than I've ever needed You before. I have nobody else to turn to, nowhere else to go. Before, I had my bank accounts to call on in case You chose not to show up. But at this moment I have to be 100 percent dependent. God, I'm giving everything over to You."

From that point on is when God started showing up. He began appearing in a big way.

I was in the valley and couldn't even see the mountaintop from my vantage point that day. All God was looking for was for me to be completely broken, He wanted my total obedience.

In my old life, I'd have money deposited into my bank account every two weeks. Now, if God chose not to show up, I couldn't feed my family or continue the mission. But as David wrote in Psalm 37: "I have not seen the righteous forsaken, nor his children begging for bread." And that was so evident in my life. Even in the hardest, darkest times that our family went through, nobody ever begged for anything. We never missed one meal, never missed a mortgage payment. Through the generosity of people who supported the ministry, our family was able to pay every bill and take care of all we needed.

But that's not to say anything came easy. I remember one Wednesday night, coming home from church. It was the end of the month, and we were two days away from all our monthly bills coming due, plus the needs of Samaritan's Feet. I was praying in my mind, "God, you've got to show up. Friday our bills are due, my mortgage payment is up and our family will be in big trouble if we don't pay it. Please, God, I've been obedient to You, I've done Your will, please don't let my kids end up homeless."

I was definitely having a heart-to-heart conversation with the Lord that night! I kept talking to Him as I was driving along, giving Him the play-by-play of my life. "Okay, God, I'm driving over to the post office where the Samaritan's Feet mailbox is. I need a miracle, God. Please help me..."

I drove out from my church, pulled onto Providence Road, all the way to the post office. When I got there, I was so scared. I didn't want to open the mailbox and be disappointed! I was pacing back and forth, just praying the whole time. "Lord, I need a miracle... please, God, show up..."

It was late, and this lady pulled up in the parking lot. And here I am, this tall, huge African guy hanging outside a post office, pacing back and forth. This woman came to check her mailbox, she was walking along looking out of the corner of her eye, probably thinking, "Is this dude going to rob me or what?"

So I figured I had to get this over with and just walk into the post office. I put my key in that mailbox, opened it up. There were two envelopes.

One of them was a bill for some ministry supplies. The other envelope was a letter from a local church that I'd never attended or spoken at, with our address written out by hand on the front. I opened it, and out tumbled a check for $3,700.

It was $40 over what our bills were for that month.

I just started to weep. I was broken. I immediately called Tracie. "You won't believe this," I said. "A church in Charlotte just sent us all the money we need for this month!"

A few weeks beforehand, we were planning Samaritan's Feet's first-ever 5-kilometer walk to be held the Saturday before Easter. We sent out announcements to different churches in the area, and we put the call out for volunteers to help organize the event.

One of the ladies who came to a volunteer meeting was a woman by the name of Deedee. She was very excited about our mission, and thrilled over what we were trying to do in the world.

I didn't realize this until much later, but on Easter Sunday, the day after our walk, there was a special offering at Deedee's church. Every year, her church chose four local non-profit organizations in the community, and split the funds for this special offering four ways. The church leaders had already chosen three non-profits, and they were trying to choose a fourth charity to bless. Providentially, Deedee walked into the room as they were debating this decision, and casually mentioned the name of Samaritan's Feet.

It's amazing how God makes things come full circle. Flashing forward to almost a year later, when I finally got the opportunity to speak at that church, I met with their missions committee about the possibility of them supporting us, and I asked them to help sponsor our worldwide efforts. I presented our vision and told them what we were trying to do.

Afterwards, one of the leaders commented, "That's wonderful, Manny, the next step is that you need to find somebody at our church who will be a champion for your cause. Get the church involved, and then we can look at what level of financial support we can provide you."

I was confused. "But wait, you don't understand," I added. "You've already supported us."

"No, Manny, we don't do that," they told me. "We have a step-by-step process that every charity has to go through when they ask us for support."

"But a year ago, you gave us $3,700," I replied. They insisted that I had to have been mistaken.

When I returned home, I told Tracie what had happened. I noted how strange the meeting had been. "They don't seem to be aware they had supported us," I said. "Isn't that odd?"

We held our second annual 5K barefoot walk in Charlotte a couple of weeks later, and I ran into Deedee there. It was then, during our conversation, that I learned she attended the church that had donated the miracle check to us a year earlier. It was the same place where I had been to this strange meeting just weeks before. "Deedee, the most unusual thing happened with your church," I told her. She asked me what I meant.

"A year ago, I was at the point in my life when I needed God to show up," I explained. "You wouldn't believe the miraculous way that God appeared, there was a large and unexplained check from your church in the mail one day. And a year later, I went and spoke at your church... and they didn't even know they had supported Samaritan's Feet. This is a great mystery."

Deedee's eyes lit up, and she laughed. "After I came to the organizational meeting for the walk last year, I was so inspired by what you shared," she said. "I wanted to find a way for us to get involved and I didn't know how. So the next day, they were looking for a charity to receive funds from our special Easter donation, and I just off-handedly mentioned Samaritan's Feet. They must have gone ahead and done it!"

My jaw dropped. A year before that moment, God's reputation was on the line with me. But He already had plans set in motion that I couldn't even comprehend. In my tiny finite mind, I was freaking out just trying to get the bills paid for my family and the ministry, praying to God to perform a miracle. I didn't realize that He had already started the machinery to make that miracle happen way ahead of time.

I'm not perfect. I've missed the mark many times in very human ways. But I am here to tell you we serve a *big* God. I can see how He has ordered our steps. I've seen the amazing things He allows to happen in this world if we only obey. It took me a long time to figure it out, but when I realized what I had to do I couldn't be a spectator any more or watch from the sidelines. I had to get in the game and say Yes.

That one word, "Yes," takes sacrifice and perseverance. If we're willing to pay the price, there is a reward. Not money or fame... nothing can compare to standing there in awe and amazement of what He's doing. I see huge companies offering us millions of pairs of shoes to distribute, and these corporations wouldn't even know this knuckle-headed Nigerian boy from Adam!

For surviving my trials I get to enjoy the privilege of seeing His hands at work, I get to see God in action every day as Samaritan's Feet acts as a conduit to help the less fortunate around the world. I get to live God's Word in my daily life, even though it took some very difficult times to become a voice for the voiceless.

When your prayers are unanswered, you might think that they've fallen on deaf ears. During your hardship, you may be tempted to feel that God has forgotten all about you. Close your eyes and imagine the Lord looking at your life from a distance, wondering why you keep holding on to your doubt, anxiety, and fear. Remember, the presence of your heavenly Father remains with you even when your life needs repair. Even when His solution is not what you seek, be assured that it is just what you need for the trials you face.

Through my testing came testimony. All those experiences and hardships my family and I endured in those early days of Samaritan's Feet formed the building blocks of faith. Now, regardless of what I'm going through in life, I know in my heart I have a God who will never leave me or forsake me.

Oftentimes, we think things will be easy when we give our lives over to God. But when a human being is called to fulfill a higher vision, the process the Lord provides is always a demanding one. Let nobody convince you that the road will not be rough. The implications of the journey are gigantic, and so are the risks. But the rewards, in turn, are amazing.

When you say "Yes" to Him, get ready for a complete transformation. A God idea will find the acceleration of the Almighty behind it, to fuel it to greatness. What the Lord does may be a surprise to us, but rest assured that He's already designed it. To us, it's like opening a box and finding all sorts of unexpected goodies inside. We can never even begin to explain the magnitude of the things He does.

If I had not gone through deep valleys, I wouldn't be as passionate, as adamant, as joyful as I am as God uses me to accomplish this huge mission.

NUGGETS OF VIRTUE

I once heard about a man from the Northeast United States who had a dream to climb Mount Kilimanjaro. He worked hard to prepare physically and spiritually for the day when he would finally ascend up that mountain and stand on its peak. His diet changed, his work ethic changed, everything about this man changed during his lengthy preparation.

A few months before he was to leave for Africa, he came down with a terminal disease and abruptly died. This devastated his wife, because she saw the commitment that her beloved husband had made to this cause, the dream he had of climbing that fabled mountain. But before he passed away, on his death bed, his wife made him a promise. "I'm going to make sure that your dream doesn't die with you," she said. "I'm going to fulfill your vision. I'm going to climb that mountain for you."

Then he passed from this life.

His wife started working out and preparing herself for the arduous task ahead. She committed to this goal in the name of showing the world what kind of man her husband was. She let nothing get in the way, nothing could shake her resolve.

The day came for her to fly to Kenya. After she landed in Nairobi, she traveled all the way into Tanzania, to the foot of the mountain. Then she and two hired guides began the dangerous trek up Kilimanjaro. They climbed, hiked, and used all the knowledge she had spent so much time studying back at home.

As they moved up the side of the mountain, the journey was getting more and more difficult. There was snow and ice, and it was becoming very cold, especially at night. She admitted to herself that she didn't expect such severe conditions and challenges. There was no way for her to properly prepare for the shortage of breath she'd encounter after passing the 10,000 feet mark.

The danger increased along with the altitude. As she drew closer to the top of the mountain, navigation became more and more treacherous, and she often felt that she was going to fall. The edges were sharp, and the path was not clearly marked. But she never gave up, because of the commitment she had made to her beloved husband. He was always at the back of her mind and deep within her heart.

After days, they inched closer to the peak where they encountered a small group of trekkers who were making their way back down the mountain. "How was the summit?" the lady asked them as they shared some food. "What was the feeling like standing there?"

"No, no," someone from the other group said. "We turned around. It was far too dangerous. One of our team members fell into a crevasse and we had to work for several hours to dislodge him with our pickaxes. We decided as a group that reaching the top wasn't worth our lives. You might want to turn around yourself, it's not worth the risk."

She didn't even think about heeding their warning. "I appreciate your advice," she said. "But if this is how God's going to take me to heaven, then so be it. I made a commitment to my husband before he died, and I'm going to reach the top of the mountain for him. I'm going forward, no matter what. If nobody else will go, I will go alone."

Because of the conditions, her hired guides chose not to continue. They decided to join the retreating hikers, leaving her all alone to finish the journey.

This was the difference: the other group of hikers undertook this trek for the sake of accomplishment. They just wanted to say they had climbed Mt. Kilimanjaro to cross it off a "bucket list" of things they had done before they died. But she had a reason that was far more noble. Her determination to succeed fueled her every step of the way up the mountain.

And she soon found out that the other team had turned around just three kilometers below Kilimanjaro's peak. They simply hadn't seen the top. Because of their fear and the anxiety and apprehension they gave into, they couldn't transcend those mental and physical barriers with a force that was bigger than themselves. Nothing was truly driving them to go further, nothing emboldened them to push beyond the danger that threatened their lives.

It wasn't more than an hour later when the determined widow reached the top of Kilimanjaro. Neither she nor the others had any idea that they were so close. She had made it, and had fulfilled the promise to honor her husband's life.

When you are committed to a task greater than yourself, it will drive you to never give up. You will reach places no one else will go. This story of sacrifice and perseverance speaks powerfully to my journey, and I have never forgotten it. Every time you want to abandon your dream, remember this. Maybe the peak of your mountain is right around the corner. Never give up or give in. Pursue your vision—the Lord is with you!

Above: As a young boy in Nigeria, with my sisters. *Below:* With Dr. Maya Angelou in New York at a Gibarron Foundation event.

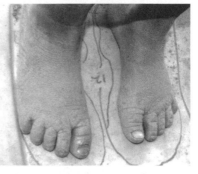

Clockwise, from top: Outfitting a boy with shoes at Chacara Indigena Tuxa in Brazil; Infected and swollen feet of a teenage boy at shoe distribution in Lilongwe, Malawi; A child in Uganda before a distribution. This shows why we do what we do. *Right, above:* Children joyful after receiving their first-ever pairs of shoes. *Right, below:* Haiti, 2006.

Above: Belem, Brazil. *Below:* Children excited to receive their first pair of tennis shoes at a school in South Africa.

Above: Wes Cruickshank, Samaritan's Feet founding board member, showing love to a child at a shoe distribution in South Africa. *Bottom:* With former NBA star Muggsy Bogues presenting the "Shoot for Shoes" trophy to our 2008 winner in Charlotte.

Left: Leading the pack to kick off the 300-mile World Walk from Charlotte to Atlanta in 2008. Above: Damien Horne, Ernie Johnson, Michael Johnson, and me in Atlanta at the finale of the World Walk. Below, JTG owner, Tad Geschickter, NASCAR driver Kelly Bires, and me at Lowe's Motor Speedway with the Samaritan's Feet No. 47 car.

Above: Washing the feet of a child in Lima, Peru. *Below:* Tracie loving on a child in Peru. *Right above:* Barefoot governors: Mitch Daniels of Indiana and WestVirginia's Joe Manchin. *Right below:* Carolina Panther C. J. Wilson at a Charlotte shoe distribution.

Far left, above: With a child in Lima, Peru in July 2009, with Karen Fairchild of Speedway Children's Charities looking on.

Far left, below: Excited children in Missouri aftrer receiving new shoes from Samaritan's Feet.

Left: With Kenny Smith, Ernie Johnson, and Charles Barkley on the set of "Inside the NBA" on Turner Network Television.

Below: The Ohonme family (l. to r.): Yemi, Dele, Tracie, Manny, Nike, and Wale.

PART 2

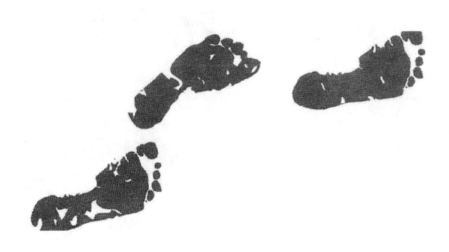

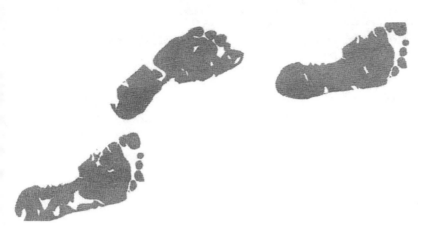

7: OBEDIENCE

From the beginning, I knew that Samaritan's Feet was going to do something sports-related. I was well aware that sports is a universal language in the world that everybody understands. From my personal childhood experience, I knew that kids need shoes to play sports!

But I didn't realize the health implications of shoes until I really researched the topic. I discovered that this was more than just games. Kids need shoes to stay *alive* in many places around the world. I did not know how many people die of preventable causes, how simple and basic foot-related infections cause millions of kids to become sick. A lack of basic medicine in these regions leads to people dying from foot-borne diseases, and many of these children are perishing just because they don't have shoes to put on their feet.

All of this was new to me at the beginning and I had much to learn in the process. At the outset, I just thought we were going to give kids shoes, wash their feet, play some sports, and tell them about Jesus and His love!

But God explained to me, "Well, that's *your* plan, Manny. I've got something *bigger* in mind."

Who knew that someday we were going to be feeding over 2,000 kids in Africa on a daily basis. There are so many orphans in Africa who have lost their parents because of AIDS and HIV; who was going to take care of them? We didn't go into this outreach thinking that we were going to make such an impact.

God always has a larger agenda, but He shows you the big picture little by little. If He had revealed everything to me at once, the entire width and breadth of this ministry... I'm telling you, I would have given up a long time ago. The thought of this much work would have been overwhelming.

I really think God unveiled pieces of the puzzle every single day, because that created a dependence on God. All He wanted was my obedience. When I said Yes, I was admitting, "Lord, I don't know what I'm doing, but I'm trusting you."

On our first trip to South Africa in 2003, we visited a settlement outside Cape Town. There were 14 or 15 volunteers who went along with my wife and me. We worked with a missions organization and a church pastor who runs a sports-based ministry on the ground there. When we arrived, we did some children's programs, we brought in clowns and games and made it really fun. We had a mini-Olympics competition and a sports-themed festival with the kids, and then we did our shoe distribution.

We brought about 1,000 pairs of shoes that first time, and I honestly don't remember why I ever thought that would be enough. When we set up, we saw a long line stretching off into the distance starting early in the morning... there had to be over 2,000 children and young people waiting for shoes.

And that's when I really knew that we were on to something big in God's kingdom. The need was so enormous, and my heart was just shattered when we ran out. I had seen that look before, those sad eyes, when I was a child in Nigeria and saw my friends who didn't receive shoes.

We were face-to-face with people who put Americans on pedestals, and we were down on our knees washing their feet. They would have been more than happy to wash ours. But we were there to serve *them*. We had traveled a great distance, and they didn't know us personally. But because of the love that we showed them, we obtained instant credibility. We were able to minister to them, to love on them, and they shared things with us that they wouldn't normally share with anyone else.

The community we visited had many Muslims living there, and we blessed countless Muslim children that day. I vividly remember one woman who brought her kids and we washed their feet, then we gave the children new shoes. We then offered to wash her feet as well and give her shoes and socks. This completely overwhelmed her and she was crying because she couldn't believe that we would touch her, that we would love her and her children in such a way.

"The only time my husband touches me is when he wants to have sex, she told us. "You are touching me because you love me, and I can feel that love because you're washing my feet."

When Christ gave us this mandate in John 13:7 about washing the feet of His disciples, it was a command and not an option. This happened late in Jesus' time on earth. Satan had just sealed the deal with Judas to betray Him. The Last Supper had been served. All the relevant instructions are laid out in that chapter: Jesus prepared a basin of water, then He washed His disciples' feet and carefully dried them.

"You don't realize what I am doing," Jesus told them. "But you'll understand later."

I remember a letter a friend of mine wrote me recently. "How do churches grow?" he began. "The answer is that they don't. I'm not saying they don't grow at all. They tend to grow to the size of the charisma of their leaders only, and no more. That's because there are two significant elements missing in the church today: touching and treating. Consider what happened with the idea of going barefoot for Jesus. The concept itself brought attention to the plight of the poor. If people went barefoot for food or medicine or food or shelter, going barefoot wouldn't make a difference. But when it involves cleaning people's feet and giving shoes, going barefoot ignites people. Why?"

"Because washing feet is a serious matter," he answered rhetorically. "Jesus said, 'Unless I wash your feet, you have no part with Me.' That's *serious business*. 'I, your Lord and teacher, have washed your feet. You should wash one other's feet too.' There wasn't an organization called Samaritan's Feet 2000 years ago."

But, thank God, there is one now.

We prayed for that Muslim woman and encouraged her. We explained that we had come to South Africa because God loved her. He had sent us to show His love.

To see her reaction, and the reactions of our team members, was so moving. As she walked away with her children in tow, she was smiling and crying. For the first time she felt like she was special—a *somebody*. She was more than just an object.

Many of the children in that community are affected by HIV, and they have become used to being forgotten and pushed to the fringe of society. In a lot of communities in Africa, people with AIDS might as well have leprosy too. They become completely untouchable. Infected men, women, and children couldn't believe that we would reach out and care about them, and touch their feet with love. Our actions just messed their hearts up!

My own life was transformed that day. God was doing major surgery on my heart. He sealed the deal with me at that moment, and I knew then I wanted to do this for as long as God would allow me to. At that moment in South Africa I had answered a call to do something far more significant than I had ever signed up for. I honestly thought we were just going there to bless people and play sports with children. I had no idea that my life was going to fundamentally change.

Our work there was finished when we ran out of shoes. I looked outside and there was still a line of families waiting. I pulled the local pastor aside. "You've got to talk to these people, brother," I told him. "They're not going to listen to me!"

The pastor looked at the crowd and couldn't believe what he saw. "Look at this monster you've created, Manny! You've created a problem for me now!" he exclaimed.

"This is just a testament that the harvest is plentiful," I replied. "The needs outweigh the resources right now. But we serve the Lord of the harvest, the One for whom all things are possible. We've just got to pray to God that He brings us more resources."

The pastor and I addressed the people in line, we told them that we'd come back again the next year by the grace of God, and that we'd bring more shoes. I shared my testimony and I prayed with them. Some of them weren't so happy, and the sadness of those children who'd been standing patiently in line for hours caused tears to well up in my eyes.

Some of them pleaded with us, "If you have a pair of shoes that aren't so good, we'll take them," one mother said. "Anything you can give, please help us."

I was blown away. "Oh, wow," I said out loud. "This is a bigger ministry than I ever envisioned."

When you are on a journey of obedience, it's a perpetual work in progress. There's no beginning, there's no termination. You've just got to immerse yourself in the process, because God's developing you daily. When things started really moving with Samaritan's Feet, when schools, churches, and individuals stepped up and supported us, that process was very much evident.

God performed miracles for Samaritan's Feet every single day. A businessman in town I knew, who was the lieutenant governor of the local Kiwanis Club, invited me to one of their functions. I went and spoke, and people were blown away by the sheer scope of what we were trying to accomplish. They asked what the organization needed, and I told them that first and foremost, we needed an office. Samaritan's Feet was quickly outgrowing both the Ohonme family home and Le Peep Restaurant.

That businessman ended up donating office space to us. We were there for a while, and eventually worked out an arrangement where we started paying some rent and taking on more of the responsibilities of ownership. But Samaritan's Feet soon outgrew that office as quickly as we moved in. People in our community helped us organize statewide drives, and we were bringing in thousands of pairs of shoes.

In the first year of our ministry, I used to have regular, informal get-togethers with this very diverse group of successful professionals from Charlotte. We prayed together, inspired each other, and we talked about our families with one another.

One guy was a former NFL and All-American football player. One was a man who once ran a chain of hotels, but remained very invested in ministry, helping the needy in the inner cities. He'd left the corporate world, like I had, and he became the executive director of one of the largest inner city ministries in Charlotte. We would discuss our visions and dreams. All of us in that group had some form of ministry going on in our lives.

During the time when Samaritan's Feet was beginning to receive many blessings, we were all sitting and praying together in one of the hotel conference rooms we use. One of the men in our group, a principal and a basketball coach, said something to me that I've never forgotten to this day. He said, "You need to pour yourself into whatever God is choosing to bless in your life."

That made me pause, and I meditated on his statement. At its conception, our vision for Samaritan's Feet was simple: shoes and sports.

"Think about it," he continued. "There are six billion people in this world. Over half of them will never be able to afford a pair of shoes. What you are doing is saving lives, Manny. Sports are these things we do and watch to keep our minds from going crazy, it keeps us focused on life. But those shoes save lives."

A light bulb immediately went off in my mind! From then on, I poured all my energy, all my excitement, all my passion into Samaritan's Feet, and I made sure it was more about the shoes than the sports.

It was an important shift in our approach. We've always been involved with sports and always will be, but instead of leading with the nebulous idea of a sports ministry, we focused on the fact that half a billion people in this world don't have shoes. Three hundred million children wake up every day without shoes on their feet, can anyone truly wrap their mind around that fact?

That 300 million number became our absolute core focus. And God blessed our "Yes," our decision of further obedience to Him.

That particular "Yes" was the catalyst for a propelling effect and we moved forward like never before. People came out of the woodwork to help our cause—schools, sports teams, and civic clubs all across the Carolinas. We touched many young people's lives with our retooled message, and it compelled a great number of them to action.

One of our first board members was the superintendent of all the Catholic schools in the Charlotte area. She gave us the chance to go into all the Catholic schools in the region and share a message of hope. We reminded those kids that we are placed here on earth for a reason. We emphasized that we all have specific responsibilities to make this planet a better place. We challenged the next generation to take up the torch and light up their world.

We had stories pouring in from elementary schools, high schools, and colleges. We heard all the exciting and creative ways of how young people were stepping forward and helping. People of all ages really responded to our cause, they wanted to know how they could get involved, how they could help. We heard about birthday parties and bar mitzvahs where there were no gifts, everybody brought shoes for Samaritan's Feet instead.

These were gifts that kept on giving!

Things were going very well, and God was doing a phenomenal work through us. Every month, we did more. We took in more shoes, completed more mission trips around the world. We were growing 100 to 150 percent every year. If you were to chart our growth, the graph would be reaching to the sky! We were doubling our efforts over and over, all for God's glory.

My friend John was a president of one of the local Kiwanis Clubs, and also an executive vice president for a logistics company in Charlotte. He came up to me after I had spoken to his group one afternoon.

"Manny, I want to help you," John said. "The regional leadership of the Kiwanis Club organization is getting together to meet next week. I'd like you to come as my guest. I want to help you make a statement, to paint a picture of what this vision is really about."

Okay, I said. I told him it all sounded great.

The meeting was in Matthews, a suburb of Charlotte. All the governors, lieutenant governors and presidents of all the Kiwanis Clubs in North Carolina were there. The meeting was called to order, and the leadership took care of some organizational business. Then it came time for the presentation that would communicate why adopting Samaritan's Feet and our Shoe of Hope projects should be a statewide initiative for the Kiwanis Club.

John, the president of the local chapter who was championing our cause, came out on stage. When he walked in, jaws dropped all around the room. He was wearing a ripped shirt, his pants were in tatters, and his feet were bare. I hadn't seen him before the meeting, I'd just talked to him on the phone for a minute. What was going on with this brother? Did something happen to him, was he alright?

John explained to the surprised group that he had been walking around the city for four hours. His purpose was to see and feel exactly what it was like to not have shoes. He had cuts on his feet. There was caked blood smeared all over his ankles. His legs and feet were so dusty and dirty, he left a trail of grey footprints on the floor as he walked.

"Here I am," John said when he reached the podium. "I represent the half billion people in this world who woke up this morning without shoes on their feet. I had to walk over six miles to get water for my family. I stepped through the glass from broken bottles. I stepped over rocks. You can look at the soles of my feet, and you can see how dirty and bloody they are."

"But I live in America, I am blessed," John continued. "I can go to the store and buy a pair of shoes to protect my feet. I can go to Rite Aid or CVS to purchase medical supplies to bandage and heal my cuts and scrapes. But over 300 million children in this world don't have those opportunities. If untreated, these cuts on my feet could lead to infections, which could then lead to amputation or even worse. Any of these kids can easily lose their lives, just because they don't have shoes."

"Can you help make Manny's vision a reality? Can you help put shoes on these impoverished children's feet?"

There was not a dry eye in the place. John certainly had everybody's attention.

All the Kiwanis Clubs in the state immediately signed on to help. All across North Carolina, local chapters raised over 20,000 pairs of shoes for Samaritan's Feet, and they took on sponsorship for our annual 5K barefoot walk. That was the beginning of a wonderful relationship with the Kiwanis Club, a great civic service organization.

NUGGETS OF VIRTUE

Someone once told me that the safest and the greatest place to be is in the dead center of God's will. This is where you can just *flow*; you've got the Creator of the universe on your team. What is there to lose, what can't you accomplish when you're in that sacred place?

Most people go through their lives wondering, trying to figure what their divine appointment is. A lot of men and women are struggling to find out what they're designed to do. It's perhaps the greatest question we humans can ask during our time on earth: "What am I placed here for, and why?"

The day that God reveals providentially what your assignment is, nothing can stop you. No force of nature can shut the door that's been opened. You are operating at peak power, all your cylinders are firing properly, and you will not be denied. God has you right where He wants you, working through you with your building blocks of commitment, faithfulness, and sacrifice. You have to walk through the full process to get to where you need to be, and on the journey you need 100 percent obedience.

I believe that obedience is the key ingredient to saying Yes. With obedience, we will never miss the providential and divine God moments that happen in daily life.

Other people might look at you and wonder, "Why does it seem like everything this person does is successful?" What they might not fully understand is that getting to that place doesn't happen overnight. There are no shortcuts to that "sweet spot" where God wants you.

The Lord is a farmer who operates in seasons. He tells us in Ecclesiastes 3 that there's a time to sow and a time to reap. All these seasons are very important to God's harvest, and no one can bypass any of them. Samaritan's Feet went through a time of planting seeds, and there was definitely a time of drought afterwards. It seemed as if God wasn't around when our family was down to its last 12 dollars. Often, in the hardest of times, I'll cry out, "God, where are you?" But I have to remember that He is right by my side. He's diverting me from making the dumbest mistakes of my life. He's saving me from choices that might ruin my potential. I love that song by Garth Brooks, "Sometimes I thank God for unanswered prayers." If God gave me everything I wanted, when I wanted it, I'd surely be in trouble!

After our drought came a season of abundance. The Lord was answering every prayer and nothing was getting in our way while we grew as a ministry. But we knew that we could never become so content that we forgot the source of all our blessings.

Regardless of the season of life you are in, God is continually teaching you and taking you through every circumstance. As long as you are obedient and faithful and remember who the Divine Author is, you can never lose. Yes, we go through winters, but God's springtime always comes, a season of renewal and growth.

Your obedience is what places you in the true center of the Father's will.

8: MIRACLES

After you donate a pair of shoes to Samaritan's Feet, an amazing chain reaction takes place.

That pair of shoes goes into one of our processing centers. Then they might be put on a ship or an airplane. They could be headed to Africa, the Middle East, Asia, the Caribbean or South America, or even somewhere in the United States. Then the shoes are in put in a car or truck, in a bag, and sent out on a shoe distribution. One of our volunteers picks that pair of shoes up after a needy child's feet are sized. We wash their feet, then lotion or anoint them with oil as we share a message of hope. Next, the shoes are placed on that child's feet, the culmination of eight beautiful minutes of shared love and compassion.

But that's the simple version of the process.

We have three warehouses strategically located across the United States (in North Carolina, Indiana and California) where we store, sort, and load shoes. At each of our facilities, volunteers from local churches, corporations, schools and civic groups help us process the shoes, and they physically touch every single pair that comes in. It's a meticulous process as we unbox the shoes, lace them up and tie them together (making sure we don't match two rights or two lefts). I sometimes wonder if the people in China and Thailand know what we do in our warehouses. Over there, they spend all these hundreds of hours stuffing the boxes with all sorts of tissue paper and packing material. Our volunteers spend thousands of hours "deboning" the shoes, removing all that dunnage!

Then we sort them by gender and size to make them mission-ready. We don't want our volunteers on the ground having to waste time with these details. We want to make sure that they can quickly and efficiently get each pair of shoes to a waiting child, ASAP. Our volunteers only have about eight minutes with each of those kids, we want to make sure they are spending every second of that valuable time loving on those children. This is why the boxes and filler paper are discarded prior to arrival in the country.

A big portion of the funds we raise helps pay for the port-to-port ocean shipping, the freight forwarding services, and the inland carriers that transport the containers between the ports and warehouses. We have an international team on our staff that takes care of all our overseas shipments. Our team helps inspect the pallets (about 320 pairs of mission-ready shoes each) and seals the containers (which can have up to 5,000 to 10,000 pairs depending on the container's size, 20 or 40 feet).

Then, the international team prepares all the proper paperwork. We partner with shipping companies and ocean carriers that help us get the containers on the water to transshipment points. Whether the shoes are going to the Middle East, Africa, or South America, our partners make sure the right shoes get to the right countries. Overseas freight forwarders that we retain work closely with our in-country partners, and help us clear the goods through customs.

In addition to all that, we have to retain the services of trucking companies that move the shipments to an in-country storage facility, whether it's a warehouse, a church, or an abandoned building. It all depends on what we have to work with. I tell people that our supply chain can be as sophisticated as we want to make it, but we always need to be very adaptable to whatever the situation is on the ground. Sometimes we're taking shoes into a location that's totally in the 21st Century, and sometimes the shoes are shipped to countries that are stuck way back in the 19th Century. In some countries, they load the shoes on trucks. In other places, it's mules and donkeys all the way!

We're trying to fully embrace the technology age ourselves. In 2009, we began looking into leveraging supply-chain logistics software that automates shipments of shoes. We'll maintain a database of incoming shoe donations so we'll know how many have been received, where in our nationwide system they are, and where each pair is going. For most of our organization's history, the majority of this information was recorded manually in Excel spreadsheets. But now, when somebody needs a specific type or size, we hope to be able to commit to those requests because we have an inventory management system. This is all just another example of the preparation that God was putting me through back in the late 1990's, when I was in the logistics software industry!

Typically, we process a container of shoes, a 20-foot or 40-foot long box, a couple of months ahead of schedule. The challenge is always local customs.

Most people don't realize how much paperwork has to go into shipments of this size. When we first begin working in a country and donate very expensive merchandise like athletic footwear to needy people (hundreds of thousands of dollars' worth of retail value), we have to convince the government that we're not coming in to sell the shoes. We want to give them away.

Different places have different procedures and different levels of difficulty. A recent shipment to Guyana was in-country within a couple of weeks after it was initially sent from America, and it was cleared with no problems. In Burundi, the president had personally invited us to come, so our shoes were received as an official and diplomatic shipment—it was brought from the ports to the warehouses by government vehicles. In cases like that, there are no issues. We get there, we train the team, and we move into action right when we hit the ground. The only thing we have to coordinate is the transportation.

Some countries follow a very regimented process of getting goods through customs. They know we're a NGO (non-governmental organization), they know we're an NPO (non-profit organization), and they understand we are there for humanitarian purposes. They want to receive the help. But our June 2009 shipment to Nigeria had arrived when our team landed, but it was held up in customs because of all sorts of red tape. We simply try to be as prepared as we can be.

In many countries, we work with missions agencies, churches, or schools as partners. We consign the shoes to them, and they receive them as a duty-free, charitable donation as a NPO because they'll be used for charitable causes. In Nigeria, our partner ProHealth receives our shipments as charitable donations to the organization. We were also able to register Samaritan's Feet in Nigeria, so in the future our operation there will be able to receive shipments with little or no difficulty. We are also now registered as an operational charity in South Africa and Brazil.

But in some areas, because humanity is always capable of great falsehoods, there are people taking advantage of the NGO and NPO status. There are those who say they are coming into the country to perform humanitarian work, but they bring in shipments in order to sell them without paying duty. So these governments that are being taken advantage of have to respond by tightening the reins, which means that honest organizations like ours are forced to endure greater scrutiny. And this always results in delays and frustration. So we just have to work through the processes (such as they are), fill out all the paperwork (and there is a lot!), and we do everything we can do to get the shoes through customs and on the feet of kids that need them.

Sometimes it doesn't matter what our non-profit status is. Even if a shipment is charitable goods, we have to pay duty. Duty is a huge form of revenue for these nations, so they don't care if we're going to give the shoes away or not. In cases like that, we have to deal with all the red tape and side-business, and occasionally it becomes very frustrating. It's not like America, where there are defined processes and you follow a step-by-step procedure. In certain places around the world, there are a lot of gray areas. People want you to grease their palms, arms and sometimes their elbows too! So when we deal with a country for the first time, we have to learn all the hoops we have to jump through, and we have to get up to speed very quickly.

When a container is delayed or we have to be creative in getting shoes into a country, we have to make some secondary plans. Occasionally, our team members have to bring in shoes as checked baggage in order to cover the first several days of field projects, so we don't have a break in the early part of our schedule. We've become experts in knowing exactly how many pounds each passenger is permitted to bring along in the cargo hold!

In some countries, the depth and nature of the corruption means that we have to go completely around the government processes. In some cases we use air cargo to ship additional supplies on the plane our team flies in on. This is always more expensive.

But we always remember that it's not about the shoes, it's about the message that gets delivered with the shoes. That's why any additional expense is justifiable; it's always worth it to take on those extra costs so that we can complete our mission.

There's a whole lot that goes into each of our trips logistically as well. We have to coordinate everything, all the mundane "small stuff" most people don't consider. The in-country volunteers and those on our traveling team must have conducive accommodations, food, and water. We have to make sure that our working environments are as clean as possible so we don't get sick. And there has to be a constant supply of bottled water, because some of these countries are very hot and humid. In some regions, we have to make sure to bring toilet paper with us! If somebody gets sick, we must have the appropriate antibiotics.

Some countries are safer than others, and there are those which are more open to humanitarian missions than others. Occasionally, we need to retain a security force to keep our volunteers and shoes safe from harm.

But most of the time, by the grace of God, everything runs smoothly. Ninety percent of our projects go like this: the container arrives, our team trains local volunteers to work with us, and by the time we leave we have a well-tuned volunteer team up and running. Then we can send future shoes and they can reach further into more rural parts of the land.

In the 50-plus nations that we currently work in, we want to train indigenous people who will carry the mission forward long after we're gone. We can wash 10 million feet and give away 10 million pairs of shoes, but it will take us decades to do that.

Someone in our office actually did the math, and they figured that at our current rate, it would take 80 to 100 years to reach our goal! I want to make sure I'm alive when this happens!

So we've been training thousands of people around the world to become our in-country, indigenous volunteer base. We train them to wash feet, to share the message of hope, and to lovingly put the shoes and socks on the feet of the children. If we replicate that process over and over again in these countries, all of a sudden we have an army all over the world.

We become a united "Air Force for Jesus," bombing nations with love!

And the children we impact become part of that army. The gift of shoes empowers them to do good and share the love of God with others. Because if we don't reach them now, the dark side will reach them instead.

You hear on the news what's happening in Rwanda and Uganda and even in the Congo, where children are targeted at a young age. Groups are turning these kids into mercenaries, human killing machines. These organizations are able to feed them and provide them with clothing. Anybody who offers compassion, that's who the children are going to model themselves after.

So we'd rather have them pattern themselves after examples that will keep them out of harm's way and out of danger. We want to lead them away from the dark and dangerous path and onto a road that will bring them closer to the Lord and a successful future.

It's all about the faces of those children when they stand up in their brand new shoes. They're suddenly two or three inches taller, but they feel 10 feet high! It's one thing to put the shoes on their feet, but it's another to inspire these kids and reach into their lives. When you come to them with love in your heart, and give them something valuable that they'd never be able to afford, their hearts are open to what you have to say. You get the chance to really talk to them on a deeper level.

I've had many team members say to me, "Manny, I just don't feel comfortable speaking publicly about my faith." But every foot-washing station is transformed into a pulpit. You get the chance to freely share a message of hope with these kids. Some people are shy: "Oh, but my faith is private." But there's something life-changing that happens when you sit in front of a child. It becomes a public thing between you and that other human being. You are so free to share and ask them very simple questions.

"What's your dream? What do you want to be when you grow up? What's the worst thing that's ever happened to you? Talk to me, tell me your story."

Then you can look them in the eye and say, "Let me tell you about the person who can heal your past, the one I guarantee you has the key to open the door to your future. His name is Jesus."

It doesn't matter if you're talking directly to them in English, or through a translator in a South American village. It's powerful to see that message spring to life.

A couple of years ago, we traveled to Peru. We were in an area called Pachahutec, north of the capital city. The town is literally built on top of sand dunes. The shanties and shacks there are put together from sticks and mats.

Nothing grows in this community and water has to be brought in on trucks every few weeks. Water is a very rare commodity in Pachahutec. When we arrived in the town, we asked a lady living there if it was possible to buy some water to wash the feet of the children. She saw what we were doing and she said, "No, no, please, the only blessing I have to offer is the water I have in this tank outside our home. If this will allow you to do what you have to do, please take it."

A gift of water may seem like nothing to us in America who have faucets all over our house, but to her this was like giving us a thousand dollars!

We came into the community to do a shoe distribution and we set up in a local church. We had committed to reach about 500 children that day, and the line stretched around the corner. They had been waiting for us since early morning, the need in that community was so immense.

Before we knew what was happening it was getting late in the day, and we were running out of shoes, so we shut down the process and began loading up the bus. But there were a few people still left outside, some who had been in line since 5 or 6 o'clock in the morning... and suddenly along came these two young boys. I didn't know what was going on until Pastor Samuel, one of our partners on the ground there in Peru, leaned in and asked me a question.

"Pastor Manny, Pastor Manny," he whispered to me. "*Dos mas?* Can we do two more?"

"If we gave shoes to these two kids, we'll have to keep it open for everyone else," I explained. "It wouldn't be fair otherwise. What about the others?"

"You don't understand," Pastor Samuel said. "These kids are the poorest of the poor. Two more, just two more."

I was looking around, and saw all the desperate faces surrounding me. I looked into the eyes of children who were devastated when they learned that they would not get shoes that day.

"Pastor," I asked in disbelief. "How can you tell the difference?"

These two children had run as fast as they could, but they were late because they were selling stuff on the street to bring money to their family. They had to fulfill their obligations and take care of their parents financially. Pastor Samuel told me that these two brothers were the most faithful attendees to the church services. But they couldn't dishonor their parents by not going to work that day.

My heart melted when I learned of this.

"No, no, don't worry," I told the translator to tell those two brothers. "We will take care of you."

The way our shoe distributions work, the volunteer in charge of sizing feet writes the shoe size in marker on the child's hand. Then a "runner" goes to the place where all the shoes are kept, and gets a pair of shoes of the correct size and gender, along with a new pair of socks. Then the runner brings the shoes and socks back to the child. We have a water basin in front of all the stations, with soap and lotion and towels.

The faces of those two brothers started to light up. Their smiles were as big as the whole church.

They had stepped into a whole different world! Here were these white Americans kneeling down, serving these little Hispanic kids like they were kings. It was the first time they'd ever interacted with white people on such an intimate level. A volunteer started washing one of these little boys' feet and asked him his name. He said he was called Julio.

"God has a plan for you and your brother," we told Julio. "He's brought us down here all the way from America to come and love you guys. He has blessed us, so we're going to bless you with a new pair of shoes."

Julio's eyes opened up wide as saucers when he saw the runner coming with those shoes. The smile on his face was unbelievable! When the shoes were placed in his hands, he clutched them tightly to his little chest. He was rocking back and forth in the chair, just hugging them while we washed his feet. He was happily singing a little song the whole time.

Next, we dried his feet, and anointed them with oil, prayed over him and finally put the new shoes on his feet. Julio started to weep, repeating the same phrase over and over. The interpreter was consoling him, wiping away his tears, and speaking to him in Spanish. We asked the interpreter what Julio was saying.

"They won't laugh at me anymore," the interpreter relayed. "They won't laugh at me anymore."

"Who laughs at you?" we asked him.

The interpreter told me that they had to rotate going to school, because they only had one pair of shoes between them. One wore them one day, and the other wore them the day after. "My brother and I share flip-flops to go to school and come to church," Julio was saying. "I was only praying to God that He would give me sandals. But God brought me this brand new pair of Nikes. Nobody is going to laugh at me and my brother any more!"

I broke down in tears.

The things that we take for granted, I thought. But the God of the Universe realized what Julio's need was, and He sent people from America to answer his prayers. We might as well have given Julio and his brother two Lamborghinis.

It isn't about the shoes, though; we're on a mission to sprinkle seeds of hope. We try to tell these kids in communities like Pachahutec that they matter, that they count, that they should keep dreaming and always strive to rise above their circumstances.

I have never forgotten that moment. I just hugged that kid, and we prayed for him. I said through our translator, "Always remember this. Someday you will be a blessing to somebody else."

In Brazil, I traveled with a group of Samaritan's Feet supporters to a flooded-out community. We had to reach the area by boat. We went from house to house, intending to wash their feet and give them shoes, to provide them with medical treatment, and offer them food and sustenance supplies. We were in one of the houses with our team, I was about to step on a plank when somebody abruptly pulled me back... they could see the water underneath the floorboards, and those boards weren't going to support my weight. "If you step on that, you're going down, Manny," they told me.

I couldn't get the horrible condition of this house out of my mind as we continued on. Human beings lived here? We went to another house and met a girl who was taking care of her younger brothers and sisters. There were no adults to be found, and there was no food in this house.

I asked her, "Where are your parents?"

"They're not here," the girl answered. "They had to take my youngest brother to a clinic, which is a day's journey from here."

It tore my heart open to see this. Our team brought them food, and we washed their feet and gave them shoes. I wish you could have seen this little shack they called a house. There were no windows, no doors, and the walls looked like they were going to cave in at any moment. This house would have been labelled "condemned" in any run-down inner city slum in the United States. Nobody would have been allowed to live there for their own safety.

When God shows us a need such as this, we dishonor Him if we simply walk by and don't try to meet that need. Our team sat together on the boat leaving that community, trying to absorb what we had just witnessed. It was so hard to fully take it all in.

I summoned our in-country coordinator and asked, "What would it take to build a home for one of those families?"

A two-bedroom home with a kitchen and a living area typically cost around $3,500 to $4,000 to erect.

I turned to our team. "Guys," I said. "Tracie and I might have been able to afford to build a whole row of these in the old days, back when I was in the corporate world. But we're going to need your help on this one."

I told them that I would commit to raise the resources to build a home for one of these families. Who else would join me?

The first hand shot up. Then the second. When all was said and done, right there on that boat, our team raised the funds to build several family houses in that community.

After we left Brazil, the homes went up one by one, but progress was very slow. Typically it took a month or so to build one, but that seemed like a very long time. I asked around and found out the reason for the delay: the carpenters all shared one hammer, and all the tools they had were rusted and antiquated. Workers would labor for a couple of hours and then take a long break, sometimes for the rest of the day. I said, "We're not taking breaks, brother, we're going to get this done!"

So we returned to the area with another team, bringing raw materials and power tools with us. We announced that we were going to build the last home in a single day. "You've got to be kidding me," the locals said to us. They were skeptical. "Are you guys nuts?"

But we finished the sixth home on the second morning we were there. It took us just a little over a day to complete the full task. It was so awesome, you should have seen the young couple that moved into that sixth house, how thrilled they were.

We called those houses Light Houses, because there was only one move-in condition for anybody who wanted to live there. They had to agree to hold regular Bible study in those homes. People from the community who moved into these houses had to understand that God loved them, so they in turn could be a blessing and share the love of Christ to others.

Samaritan's Feet generally goes into a community with a very simple focus: we put shoes on people's feet and pray to God to open their hearts. We can't do everything for everybody, but there are strategic things that God allows us to accomplish, and we've been able to really step in and help in cases like this.

I remember going back to this community in 2007. The lady who lived in the first house we visited saw us approaching and she ran as fast as she could to meet us. She was so proud, and she wanted to show off her beautiful home! She was hugging and kissing us, and she told about the gatherings she'd hosted in her home. She showed us the vegetable garden she'd started growing.

Seeing how these miracles literally change people's lives is powerful. As we went from home to home, no words can describe those reunions. We saw how God used a small seed of inspiration, how He had challenged us to meet a basic need by showing that need to us.

We had been doing a lot of work in a Haitian oceanfront community called Les Cayes. One day in February 2005, a small team and I traveled ten miles south of that city to a town called Torbeck. It was the first time we'd taken a mission team to that area of the country, and we marveled at how incredible the landscape was: beautiful beaches, palm trees, and lush vegetation. The only drawback was that everybody lived in rundown shacks. It was the reverse of what it's like in the United States—wealthy residents don't like to be by the ocean in this part of Haiti, because that's where the poor people live.

To get to Torbeck, our vehicle traveled through some back country, through rows and rows of maize. We showed up on the other side of the fields to find the town, where the local missionaries and pastor were waiting to greet us.

The first thing we noticed when we pulled into the village is that there were hardly any children anywhere on the streets, maybe one or two. But within five minutes, we had 300 or 400 children crowding around us. I have no idea where they all came from. Where had they been hiding?

"Holy smokes," I said to the pastor. "Did they smell the sugar?"

When we first show up for a shoe distribution, we organize a children's program. We sing songs, tell stories, and I get to share my testimony with the kids. In some cases, a trained volunteer shares my story. We always tell them to go for the big dream. While all this is going on, other volunteers are setting up the washing stations and organizing the shoes in piles according to size and gender. In 15 to 20 minutes, we're ready to be fully operational.

One of our favorite Haitians was there—his name is Doodoo— and he was running security, protecting us as we set up. He's a really big man, almost twice as big as me! If there is ever any trouble, you definitely want Doodoo on your team. One look at him and the bad guys know they're in for more than they ever bargained for.

After the children's program, we lined all the kids up in an unfinished building behind the local church in preparation for the shoe distribution. As we got started, one of our team members named Peter Reike had a little barefoot girl in a tattered red dress come to his washing station.

She approached, and Peter smiled at her, he was trying to be so friendly and loving. "How are you?" he inquired with true compassion, trying as best he could to communicate with this little Haitian girl.

139

She screamed!

It was so loud that everybody stopped what they were doing: Doodoo and myself and all the volunteers and everyone in line. We all turned around to see what was going on.

Louis, our host minister, was serving as one of our interpreters that day. He rushed over to the scene and caught the little girl in his arms as she tried to run away. He started talking to her in Creole. We all asked, what's she saying?

"I'm scared, I'm scared," Louis translated.

Louis tried to console this little girl. "These people love you," he told her. "They've come a long way to wash your feet and give you a new pair of shoes."

Louis calmed her down, and gave her a little piece of candy. She became very quiet. The runner brought the shoes and socks. Peter went through the process of washing her feet, rubbing them with lotion, and placing new socks and shoes on her feet. After we finished praying for her, she smiled and hugged Peter.

Afterwards, Peter and I asked Louis what that screaming scene was all about. Why was she so frightened?

"You were the first white person she'd ever laid eyes on," Louis explained. "And you touched her with love. You've just changed that kid's life forever."

Imagine that you live in a remote region in Africa or South America, forgotten by the rest of the world. A stranger comes all the way to your village and tells you that God has a plan for your life. If we arrive and seek to inspire you, there's a pretty good chance that you'll take us at our word at that moment. In this 10-minute timeframe of your life, you're on top of the world. This is what we want to be able to tell everybody we meet on these trips—that they're special in God's sight and He wants to perform miracles through them.

In the Amazon region in Brazil there was a man who was a fisherman by trade. School was about to start, and he prayed that God would provide him with enough money to buy sandals for his children to wear to school.

Lo and behold, Samaritan's Feet showed up several days later with Nikes. After we finished our distribution, this man was crying. He had no idea that we were coming, and we certainly didn't know he was there praying for someone like us to arrive.

"You pray, but you don't think that God really answers," he told me. "All I asked the Lord for was flip-flops for my children, so they could walk to the schoolhouse. But He exceeded my expectations and gave them the most expensive tennis shoes, ones that would cost me a year's salary. If God can hear a poor fisherman's prayer here in the depths of the Amazon, I believe that He can do great things for anybody."

A wise man once told me, "Your future is God's history," and I never forgot that quote. When we pray, we tend to ask the Lord to do certain things. "God," we might say. "If You're really who You say You are, would You please do this or that to get me out of this bind? Would You perform this certain thing for me so I can provide for my family?"

All of this time we call "the present" has already passed on His clock. The dynamics of space and time blow my mind and it's awesome to consider what God's really up to. Sometimes I think of the Lord as a master chess player. He's always a few steps ahead of us.

Let me give you a prime example of this dynamic. Beth, a family friend who attends a church near where we live, is from a well-to-do family in Charlotte. She has a heart for the Guyanese people, and in 2006 she wanted to sponsor a mission there. She needed a compassion-based ministry to tie in with.

"We'd love for Samaritan's Feet to do a distribution to Guyana," Beth said. "I'll fly you to South America. Would you meet us there?"

We didn't know a single soul in Guyana. But we knew one thing: God always makes a way.

And as I know all too well, that way is rarely an easy one. Jai, the missionary that we were supposed to help, was robbed at knife point the night we got there. He knew the area well but had been living elsewhere for 10-plus years, and was just returning to answer God's call to serve the people of Guyana. He had forgotten how dangerous the local bus stations could be at night.

Three men stole Jai's bags, which contained his passport. So we had to wait there in the city longer than expected while he replaced his passport at the embassy, and the bus that was supposed to take us over the river and out of the city left without us.

Our return date was set. With that compressed timeframe, we had to think on our feet, and fast. When we connected with the embassy, the staff put us in contact with a person who then put us in touch with another person, and then through a complicated maze of ministers and rotary clubs, we finally were in touch with a high-ranking government official who allowed us to ship a container of shoes into the country.

We didn't know anybody when we arrived, but God had ordered and ordained our steps. Now, since that first trip to Guyana, we've sent three large containers of shoes into that country, and have been able to spread out into more rural areas with shoe distributions. We've trained local volunteers to continue the work, and have made a huge impact in that impoverished nation.

When you say "Yes" and choose to be obedient to God, sometimes the path is not very clear. But the Lord already sees what's in the future. "Just surrender," He says. "I'll take care of the rest." I could have easily become frustrated with our delays and gone ahead with other projects, but I chose to take the "Yes" path instead. Over half the population of Guyana is non-Christian, and they don't want anything to do with God, but we're now able to make a real difference there. All it took was a small delay and a detour in plans.

It wasn't the last detour in Guyana that led to a miracle. In 2008, a Samaritan's Feet team was heading back to the capital city of Georgetown from the nation's interior region. They had just completed a three-day, multi-project initiative in Guyana's remote areas, where they touched many people. But they were tired, reflecting on all that happened. To be honest, they were all a little distraught.

One of the communities they visited, they showed up with an expectation that there would only be 300 people to serve. But when they reached their destination, 700 people were waiting for them. They ended up not doing any projects that day because they didn't want to disappoint or break the hearts of 400 children. It was a hard decision to make, but necessary, so as not to create a rift in the community between the haves and the have-nots.

That night, they were thinking about what had transpired as they crossed the Berbice River on a small ferry boat. There were others on this boat with them, including a woman who was nine months' pregnant; she was being transported to a hospital in Georgetown. All of a sudden, a cry went up. "This lady's in labor, she's in labor," someone yelled out. "Is there any doctor, any nurse? Help!"

It turned out that JoNell Mahoney, one of the female members of our team is a medical doctor. Another team member, Kathy Bruce, who had gone on multiple missions with us, had just retired and so happened to be a nurse. So God had the perfect people in place on that team in order to assist her.

They led the woman to a bench on the upper deck and then prepared for the birth. JoNell and Kathy didn't have much material to work with, but they laid out towels and started leading the pregnant woman through the process. Bruce Bodman, our missions director, held a flashlight so that they could see. There was a lot of danger in this process; the bench was just two inches from the rail, and everybody prayed that the baby wouldn't fall over the side and drop into the rushing water!

Finally, after 9 p.m., the baby arrived into this world, safe and sound. The father was not there on the boat, so one of our team members did the honors and cut the umbilical cord. All the anxiety and all the regrets about the unaccomplished missions of the day just fell to the side. Everybody's focus shifted to this precious life that had just entered the world.

Those who were involved in that special moment still talk about it. This was one of those unique moments where a Samaritan's Feet team was part of something it didn't bargain for... but God wanted to show Himself as our Creator that night.

In spite of what they considered disappointment and failure in their own little world, in spite of the feeling that they could not meet the needs of some of the villagers, God had a greater need. He wanted our team to bring a new life into the world. I remember Bruce calling me when they reached Georgetown. I could hear the excitement in his voice. I told him that I didn't know that God was calling Samaritan's Feet to be a maternity ward as well as a ministry!

Bruce and another team went back to that community in 2009, and gave

143

shoes to over 2,000 children during a two-day period. Using the connections we had built four years earlier, we worked with the country's health department and prime minister's office to pull off an effort that included over 40 churches. Over 200 volunteers sized and ran and washed feet in four locations around the area. Those churches put their denominations aside and they deeply touched this community with love.

Since we first arrived in Guyana, we've left an indelible mark on over 30,000 people. And we're also working to make sure that the Guyanese people have the provisions to be an active part of God's plan. In 2008, we started a micro-finance program with 20 pilot families. Each one gets a certain number of chicks to raise, and then we build the pen for them, and we provide the medicine and feed. Their responsibility is to sell a portion of them, keep a number for themselves, and give a percentage of them to the needy of their community.

This exercise teaches them to have a source of income, combat their starvation, and act as a model of compassion in their fellow man. Each of those chicks is a loan from Samaritan's Feet, and they must pay that loan back over the course of a year and a half. We then use those paybacks as a means to get other families involved with the program.

There is a famous Eastern proverb that says: "Give a man a fish and he will eat for a day; teach a man to fish and he will eat for a lifetime." God may continue to bless us with huge donations of shoes from the likes of Nike, Adidas, Converse, Fila, Kmart, and all these huge companies, but I believe that the time is going to come when we have to build an engine to bring real economic development in these impoverished countries that we visit and bless with our shoe distributions.

Our true goal is to lift people out of poverty, not just to give them physical gifts. We want to be in the business of giving hand-ups, not handouts. We can fulfill a short-term need with a pair of shoes, and show them the love of Christ, but then they need to use God's inspiration to be able to sustain and provide for their families. And I believe that's a real long-term strategy for Samaritan's Feet: to help these people make sustainable futures for themselves.

The endgame for us is to open a shoe manufacturing plant somewhere in a third-world country. Imagine that. The day when the people that we're blessing right now can walk into that plant and watch the first shoe roll off the line.

Then they'll be able to sell those shoes and raise money for their families, and for their kids' education.

This is my dream. I want to manufacture a Samaritan's Feet shoe not just in China, but on the continent of Africa, or the jungles of South America, or wherever it is that the Lord leads us.

I pray that someday we are able to help bring about this miracle.

I would love to be there, just once, at somebody's house after a shoe distribution. I always wonder what the conversation is like when a child arrives home and their mother sees that brand new pair of shoes that she'd never be able to afford herself. Tears, rolling down her eyes, because her son or daughter now owned something that she'd never be able to buy for them.

"Oh, Pedro," I can hear her saying. "Where did you get those beautiful new shoes?!"

"Mom!" he might exclaim. "These people from America came and told me that God loves me! They told me to dream! *Sueño, Pedro, sueño!* And they washed my feet, and said there is hope for me. There's this guy in heaven they told me about named Jesus, who loves me and has a plan for my life. These people anointed my feet and put this pair of shoes on me. They told me that I could become somebody, and someday bless other people."

They will remember this experience for the rest of their lives. They may not always remember the name of the person who washed their feet, but they will always remember those eight minutes when they were loved and treated like royalty.

NUGGETS OF VIRTUE

My pastor once said this to me: "When God gives someone big visions, he also brings the provisions. The joy of God is that He gives givers gifts to give."

This is so true. Once He gives you that gift to give, the recipient knows that there is someone who cares about them and their well-being. When we offer a child a pair of shoes, there's a love that transcends the actual physical gift. Imagine the imprint that is left on that young life with they know and see that you truly care.

When you share your best with the world, it lets people know there's somebody who loves them. But then you have the opportunity to flip the tables. "It's not about me and what I can give you," you can say. "It's about the One who created both you and me. We can give Him glory through the things we do."

I believe that God intends to heal the nations. I know that He cares for all His children, that He wants to meet the needs of the poor and heal the sick. I believe that God wants us to walk by His side in this world.

I know in my heart that God intends to make supernatural provisions available to all of us. He's just looking for obedient vessels willing to say Yes.

We try so hard not to sound too preachy on our missions, but we take great care to incorporate the essence and principles of our Lord in the short moments we have with each child. Saying "Yes" is not a requirement for receiving a gift of shoes from Samaritan's Feet. But in a small and subtle way, those shoes point the wearer's footsteps back to God. Because He is the One who makes all of this possible.

Our mission and our strategy is embodied by the three "T's" that Christ taught us: teaching, touching, and treating. A friend of mine said it best: "The beauty of what Samaritan's Feet does is that you don't have to tell people you're a Christian organization. That's because you guys are allowing people to perform Christian acts of mercy and love, demonstrating what Christ did. The symbolic act alone of washing feet is so Christlike, so humbling, and so loving. It's going to be difficult for people to say No to this, Manny, because this is love in action."

146

9: TRANSFORMATION

At first, I didn't know Dr. Ski Chilton from Adam! He and his wife signed up to go with a Samaritan's Feet team to White River, South Africa, to work along with our group of 25 volunteers.

Dr. Ski was going to South Africa with no expectations. He's a scientist and a successful businessman who runs a nutritional supplement company called Gene Smart Health. He told me later on that he was seeking to be on a trip where he wasn't in charge. He just wanted to serve.

Two or three days into the journey, we sent the team to a banana plantation to perform a shoe distribution. All the workers there were black South Africans that toiled in the field all day, picking bananas. While they worked, their children were watched by a couple of helpers, who were overwhelmed by the sheer numbers. There were over 200 kids in this small enclosed playground where they were supposed to stay entertained all day while their parents worked. You should see how filthy and dirty these children were—their faces covered with snot, their clothes ripped and tattered, no shoes on their feet. It looked more like a dog pound than a playground.

Dr. Ski arrived on site and surveyed the situation. He looked at how dirty the kids were, and thought, "No way in my lifetime can I put my hands on any of these children. I don't think I'd even touch those kids with a 10-foot pole. What if they have incurable meningitis or other contagious diseases? I'm not willing to take the risk."

He tried as hard as he could to stay on the periphery. He avoided eye contact with the children and tried to blend in inconspicuously in the corner of the playground.

But then something amazing happened to Dr. Ski and he didn't know what hit him.

"Manny, I've been a Christian for over 31 years," he testified to me afterwards. "But for the first time in my life, I audibly heard a voice speaking to me. It said, 'Who are you?'"

And then, before he could recover from the shock, he heard the voice again. "*Whose* are you?"

He was frightened. Immediately, he stooped down low and picked up the child closest to him, a small baby. Before he knew it, he started rocking this little child in his arms. Out of the blue, he started singing.

"I hadn't heard that song for years," he told me later. "But I began singing the lullaby that my mom used to sing to me when I was a kid." He grabbed some towels and started to wipe the grime from the child's face. Dr. Ski was completely taken back with emotion.

"God forgive me," he kept repeating. The rest of the team settled him down, but he couldn't let the kid go. Others had to peel that child from Dr. Ski's hands before our team was able to start the shoe distribution process.

The child the doctor picked up that day was nine years old, but he looked like he was four. The malnutrition problem is so severe in that area that the bodies of these children don't develop properly. God convicted Dr. Ski and he couldn't get that picture of the child out of his mind.

After the distribution was over, our team left the banana plantation and we returned to our base. "Manny, I've got to talk to you," Dr. Ski said. He shared with me the story of what had just happened to him that day.

"My heart is aching," he told me. "These kids don't have anything. To see children with nothing, and then to see kids who are nine, ten, eleven years old look like they're five, six or seven because they don't have proper food to eat... I would never have seen or known about this unless I'd come here to wash their feet."

In that community, there are many orphans whose parents are dead from HIV and AIDS. Kids in their early teens become head of their households, totally in charge of taking care of five or six smaller brothers and sisters. That same evening, a group of those teenagers came to speak to our team. They told us their stories and made us aware of what was taking place in their community. They shared with us that an organization from Sweden that had been supporting them had run out of funding, and that they'd be pulling the plug shortly thereafter. This charity had been providing them with their one and only meal every day.

We came to give them shoes, to bless them with a message of hope, but we knew we were being called to do more. We envisioned what these boys and girls had the possibility of becoming. These were the potential lawyers, doctors, and leaders of South Africa, and we could not just sit by as they suffered without food.

We decided that we'd get together when we returned to America, and make some decisions about how we could help.

Throughout the week we were in White River, after Dr. Ski heard that voice, he was a completely different man. During each of our shoe distributions, he was getting on his knees. He was washing feet, hugging and loving kids. Then, for a week after he returned to the United States, he couldn't find rest. He would wake up at 3 a.m. every morning.

He sought counsel from Stu Epperson, one of his associates. "I haven't been able to sleep since I returned from South Africa," Dr. Ski told him. "I can't get that picture of those children out of my mind."

Stu replied, "Well, I hope that God won't allow you to sleep until you come up with a solution."

This was tough love. "That's not what I came here to hear!" Dr. Ski exclaimed. "I just came for some comfort."

Dr. Ski did some research. He learned that without quick action, malnutrition in Africa will be at a catastrophic breaking point in the next 10 to 12 years as the orphan population explodes. Every night as he was tossing and turning in bed, he asked God to give him direction on what to do. Through that process, he formed a basic concept.

"What if I came up with a nutritional supplement for those children in South Africa?" he wondered. "What if I could help orphans across that continent with something that will help nourish them and allow their bodies to grow normally?"

Dr. Ski approached the board of directors at Gene Smart Health. "We have to do something big for these orphaned children in Africa," he said. "I feel called to create a therapeutic food for these kids."

"And I need your help," he continued. "All the foods that are considered bad in the diet of the children in this country, those are things that kids over there need. Those children need fats and sugars to stay alive. We also need to add certain vitamins to this mix, because these kids are not developing fast enough. If only you could see what I've seen."

The board enthusiastically agreed, and the company started a new division called Gene Smart Compassion. The vision for this new venture was not only to create therapeutic foods and help impoverished kids all over Africa, but to leave a lasting footprint on the lives of orphaned children all across the world.

Other businessmen got involved to raise enough funding to put together a prototype. The food has now been fully tested in India, and the long-term goal is to someday create a manufacturing plant in South Africa that will make this food. Gene Smart Compassion launched internationally in the summer of 2009.

And there's more to the story.

Dr. Ski's son, Josh Chilton, was one of the best and most gifted football players in North Carolina. On the day of the 2003 state semi-final play-off game scheduled against West Charlotte in Winston Salem, while driving from a friend's house, he got involved in a head-on car accident going home to get ready for the game that evening. The accident paralyzed him from the neck down. After he lost the ability to walk, Josh gave up the will to live. He wanted to die. He really wanted to end it all.

When his father returned from Africa, Josh saw how his dad's life had radically changed from the experience. Something clicked inside him too —he was divinely inspired. "If my dad could find that kind of passion and drive from helping orphans," he thought. "I want to get involved."

Dr. Ski brought Josh to meet with me one day for lunch. Josh was so pumped up. "How can I help you, Manny?" he asked. "Just tell me how. I'll do anything."

When we brought another group of people to South Africa in 2009, we began a new mission to start building homes for some of these orphan-headed households. So what Josh is doing now is spearheading a concept called "Heroes Helping Heroes." He mobilizes high schools, middle schools, college fraternities and sororities, civic groups, basketball and football teams to help adopt different families in these regions.

He challenges each to raise $5,000, a sum that will help build a home for one orphan-headed family in South Africa. This money will also buy a meal for five children every day for a year. It will also give each of those orphans two pairs of shoes, as well as funding to learn a trade or go to school.

And none of this would have ever happened if Dr. Ski had not been obedient, saying "Yes" and gone to White River, South Africa. He went to wash the feet of orphans and to give them the gift of shoes that they could never repay. Ski said "Yes" to those children, in spite of every human inclination to say "No."

His "Yes" set off a chain reaction of love.

It's amazing to see radical changes in people's lives, how their worlds are turned upside down. Soon thereafter, I took Dr. Ski and Josh to lunch in Charlotte. During the meal, Josh went off to the restroom for a moment.

That's when Dr. Ski looked in my eyes and said, "Manny, a month ago I thought I was going to lose this boy. Now look at how passionate he is, trying to help those kids in Africa and bring hope to the hopeless."

Fernando was a homeless man in an impoverished area in Lima, Peru. He was one of those individuals who wanders around town all the time, destitute and desperate. Nobody wanted to have anything to do with him.

When we first saw Fernando, he was a horrible sight. He was wearing two or three pairs of high-water sweatpants on top of each other, he had a dirty bandana on his head. Honestly, he looked to us like he was high on drugs.

We were doing a shoe distribution in Pachahutec that day. While in transit, we were stopped at a local church to pick up some of our volunteers and Spanish interpreters. That's when we saw this guy hunched over near the church building.

One of our staff members, Vic, noticed his feet. In this ministry, we end up looking at people's feet more than we look at their faces, and we get to be pretty good at sizing people on sight. He saw that he had two old mismatched shoes (neither of them had laces), and that they were in such a dilapidated state that the tops were split open.

"Manny," Vic said. "I think this guy's probably a size 11. Do you think we can give him a pair of shoes?"

"Absolutely," I replied.

So he ran to the back of our bus, opened the cargo hold, and grabbed a pair of size 11's and a pair of size 10's too (just in case). Vic wanted to give the shoes to this man right away, but I stopped him.

"We've got to go talk to this guy," I said.

So I took one of our interpreters over to where he was, and I stooped down. At first, the interpreter couldn't believe that I wanted to talk to this person. I started by asking his name. I inquired as to what Fernando was going through in his life, what kind of challenges he was facing, and why he looked the way he did. He was sitting on the ground, looking dejected, and his shoulders were hunched over. He was miserable.

The people on the street were starting to gather and whisper. What's going on here, they wondered, What are these American guys doing? Why in the world are they talking to Fernando? The doorflaps started opening in all the shanty houses, as people looked out on the scene.

I was ministering to Fernando through the interpreter. "We'd like to bless you," I told him.

"What do you mean?" he asked. He didn't seem very impressed, he just kept staring at the sidewalk.

"We want to bless you with a new pair of shoes," I replied.

I noticed a little glimmer of light in his eyes as his curiosity peaked. "Are you serious?"

I nodded yes. "But we don't just want to give you a pair of shoes," I said. "We want you to give us permission to wash your feet."

"No, no, no," Fernando answered. "My feet are dirty. Please don't touch me."

"It would be an honor," I told him. "Please, we have come here to serve you."

Finally, reluctantly, he gave us permission. One of our team members ran quickly to fetch a water basin, grabbed a towel from inside the church. And right there, while I was talking to him, we washed his feet.

As we ran the soap and water over his toes, he was overcome with emotion. He was sobbing and crying. Nobody had ever touched him like that before. Some local residents told me later that Fernando was incredibly cold-hearted, that he never smiled or talked to other people.

"Fernando," I asked him, "Did you know that God sent us here just for you?"

"No, it can't be," he said, still sobbing. "God doesn't even know I exist."

"Yes, He does," I insisted. "He loves you so much, He sent this team of American missionaries here. He wanted to remind you of His love for you."

We anointed Fernando's feet with oil, dried them off, put new socks on, and placed new shoes on his feet. And there, on the sidewalk near that church, Fernando gave his life to Christ.

When I looked up, a crowd was gathering. More and more people were looking out of their houses. I addressed them through the translator.

"I'll bet that none of you thought something like this could happen in this community," I said. "God had to use Fernando to stop us in our tracks. If any of you assembled here are thinking this is just about Fernando, it's not. It's about you."

Just from the power of what they had seen and experienced, seven other men and women in that crowd gave their lives over to the Lord. They saw a demonstration of love that day and wanted to be a part of that picture. If this God could love such a person as Fernando, they also wanted to know that love. We prayed for them there on that street made out of sand.

But the story continues. One of our team members handed Fernando some money to go get something to eat, with no other intention than to simply bless him.

"Can you wait here for a moment?" Fernando asked.

Then he dashed across the street and we didn't know what was going on. A few minutes later, he came back with a liter bottle of orange drink and some plastic cups. He gestured to us to each take a cup.

"Would you celebrate with me?" Fernando asked us. "You are my new friends, and I want to celebrate with you. Nobody ever showed me such love, and I want to thank you."

His hands were still dirty, but we didn't care. We had a small celebration of communion with Fernando that day, right there in the street.

The next night we were scheduled to hold a crusade meeting in a local stadium. Fernando arrived, and he was cleaned up, wearing a new outfit. The pastor couldn't believe what he saw. I couldn't believe it either; I literally walked right past him at the crusade meeting, I didn't even recognize him! He had to stop me to get my attention!

Fernando came early to help set up the chairs, and he was the last one to leave. And I saw his joy as he worked so hard to make that meeting come off without a hitch. His story is one of the highlights of everything that God's allowed me to be involved in, on this walk that we call Christianity.

There was an attorney who went with us on that team. She was skeptical at the beginning of the mission, but her life was changed from that moment on. It was truly a manifestation of what the Bible says: "When a sinner is in Christ, he is a new creation." We all saw a real live transformation into a new creation, right there in the eyes of a man named Fernando.

There's a pair of young men I want you to meet. I originally met them in an orphanage in Nigeria when we were there to put shoes on their feet.

Ibrahim is from northern Nigeria. His father was a Muslim. At the age of 16, Ibrahim was planning to disrupt and bomb a local Christian church with his friends. They went there with destruction in mind, but when he stepped inside that church, Ibrahim recalls that the Holy Spirit arrested him. He was completely frozen in place, he couldn't do anything. Then he felt this urge to run. When he finally came back to that church, he attended a service and came forward at the altar call. That day, he gave his life to Christ.

Ibrahim's father was one of the leaders of that community's Muslim sect. Somebody told him what had happened to his son at the church, and when Ibrahim's father heard this news, he kicked his child out of the house. His outraged father attempted to kill him by tying him up and stabbing him with a knife, but he managed to escape and run away. The church took him in, tended to his wounds, and transported him to safety. He grew up in a Christian orphanage called Gidan Bege, or "House of Hope."

This is where we met him. At the time of our shoe distribution at that orphanage, he had been living there for five years and was finishing high school. He was wearing worn-out flip-flops, and we gave him the first pair of tennis shoes he ever owned.

I got to play soccer with him and I just fell in love with this young boy, with his determination and his zeal for life. I asked him what he wanted to be, and he just looked back at me and said, point-blank, "I want to be like you."

I could tell that this was a young man who was going somewhere, but Ibrahim's dreams were grand. He wanted to become a missionary, to reach Muslims and help them to renounce violence just as he had. But God brought Samaritan's Feet to his door that day. When I returned to America, I found an opportunity for him to go to a missionary training school in South Africa through YWAM (Youth With A Mission). My wife and I pledged to help sponsor Ibraham. And we sent him to the YWAM facility in South Africa, where he finished his education.

Then his desire was to come to the U.S., to Orlando, Florida, and take part in an advanced program that taught him how to preach. We helped him with that too. He's excelled so much that he's now one of the instructors at that facility, and he's lived here in the United States for four years. He's teaching people how to reach Muslims through sports, and organizing outreach initiatives all around the world.

I'm so very proud of Ibrahim and feel as if he is my own son. I talk to him once a month and every time I hang up the phone I think about the implications of my decision to say Yes. What if I'd said No to going to Nigeria, No to helping Ibrahim? Here's this amazing kid who's completely turned his life around into something incredible and productive—because somebody chose to believe in him.

Gabriel was living there in Gidan Bege too. He was a street kid who had never been rescued and had no family. When we met him and put shoes on his feet, he and Ibrahim were two of the older kids in that building, acting as role models and leaders for the younger ones. They were glad to have a home, and were able to do the things they wanted to do, but there was no path for either of them that led out of that situation.

Gabriel wanted to do the same thing, to be a missionary. He ended up going to South Africa too. Now he lives in Switzerland, where he's a worship leader, a guitarist, and a truly anointed singer. And as a testament to God's miracles, in the past year Gabriel found his family and has been able to reconnect with them.

He's just a phenomenal man, but when we first met Gabriel, there was no bridge between him and his dreams. Now we're sponsoring him. He's going to be married to a Norwegian girl (which is ironic—Tracie is part-Norwegian!) and he's studying to earn his bachelor's degree. Gabriel wants to be a videographer and create documentaries to show the world what's going on in Africa. His heart burns for his home country and continent, and he wants to shine a light on everything that's happening there.

Gabriel came and stayed with us in Charlotte in 2009, so we were able to pray with him and encourage him. His dream is to enter seminary full time, and we're going to support him and help him pay for tuition. He told me once, "I want to reach the world like you reach the world, Manny."

This is exciting to me. That is full-circle!

God, in His infinite and providential way, brings people into one's path

156

at exactly the right time. We were fortunate to be the connection to help these two young men transform their lives and live their dreams, to create paths where there were none before. There are many, many more Gabriels and Ibrahims out there, who are just one "Yes" away from having their incredible potential unlocked. If we choose to be available to what God wants to do through us, we can transform their lives... and become transformed ourselves in the procces.

In Burundi, I saw a group of people who thought they were forgotten. These were people who were chased from their homes during a civil war in that nation. Their houses were burned down and they were left with nothing. Before they were displaced, some of them were farmers, or ranchers, or successful businesspeople. All of a sudden they were homeless and shoeless, without enough food to eat. Many were orphaned or widowed. Families were separated and dispersed across refugee camps in neighboring countries; they had gone from comfortable daily routines to small houses made of straw in Congo and Rwanda. They had become foreigners overnight.

The genocide in Burundi came about because of conflicts between the Hutu and Tutsi tribes. There is also a third group in Burundi, the Twa, who are pygmy people. All three groups had been living in peaceful unison until the Tutsis decided that they wanted to banish all the Hutus from the country. Tutsi extremists assassinated the democratically elected Hutu president in 1993, and people who had previously loved each other immediately became enemies. Friends, neighbors, even married couples all started killing each other. Innocent children were caught in a web of hatred and violence, not knowing whether to choose mom's side or dad's side, and so they were left alone in the dark.

This war raged for 12 years.

There has been peace in Burundi since 2005. Some of those families are coming back to their homeland to help heal the nation. Burundian president Pierre Nkurunziza has spent the first four years of his presidency fostering reconciliation, telling the citizens that together, the country can overcome all obstacles and hardships. Divided, they will be destroyed.

In August 2009, Samaritan's Feet accompanied President Nkurunziza to visit some of these families and to show them that they mattered to God—no matter if they were Hutu, Tutsi or Twa. The President addressed them, "We're going to kneel down on this dirty floor and pray for you. We're going to wash your feet and give you a new pair of shoes. I know you'd never be able to afford these shoes, and we don't expect you to ever pay us back. You are so valuable to God that He wants to bless you through us."

I'll never forget the sparkle in their eyes when these former refugees heard this message, when the leader of the country got down on the floor and washed their feet. I know the light of hope was switched on in their hearts. As he washed their feet, President Nkurunziza encouraged them: "Hang in there, keep going. Don't give up. God is on your side."

This was a mutual transformation; it was not one-sided at all. People think serving is a matter of blessing others, but that's not true. Mutual transformation occurs when you help other people—you see who you are as an individual, and you know that it's only by the grace of God that you are blessed. You get to be the hands and the extension of God to impart that blessing on somebody else, a feeling that transcends anything you've ever envisioned. You yourself are on the receiving end of that blessing too.

This is what I have experienced.

The president's heart was touched when he saw these thousands of people who showed up early to meet with us. They didn't know what they were getting that day until we arrived. We gave them shoes and socks, we knelt down and loved them. We gave each of those people eight minutes of dignity and love, and we showed them that they mattered. They will never forget that for the rest of their lives, and neither will President Nkurunziza.

One of my previous pastors said that the definition of a leader is not one who stands on top of a mountain and beckons to his followers to come. A leader is somebody who goes all the way down to the bottom of that mountain, who grabs the people one at a time by the hand. "Follow Me, walk beside Me." That's what Christ modeled to us 2000 years ago. To this day, He brings us alongside Him.

President Nkurunziza started out washing the feet of a Hutu, then a Tutsi, then the feet of a Twa. Then Hutus started washing the feet of Tutsis. Tutsis washed the feet of Hutus. Over and over, a simple mutual act of kindness was repeated, one that said, "We are the same, we are one nation, under God's banner of love. I love you enough that I'm willing to humble myself and serve you."

It was an amazing scene to behold, a divine picture of genuine compassion. To think that a decade ago they were killing each other. Now they were washing each other's feet in the name of God's love.

One of the women we interviewed was a former refugee who had just come back from the Congo. She was so moved that the president had brought his friends from all over the world to bless her. "We were not forgotten," she kept saying. "We were not forgotten."

NUGGETS OF VIRTUE

With the total transformation brought on by saying Yes, we have a responsibility to enjoy the experience. The gift is in the journey. When you're going through the process of surrender and complete obedience, you might say, "Why do I have to go through all this struggle and undertake these challenges, I've already said 'Yes' to the One who created it all!"

The fact of the matter is that the journey is one of the greatest gifts God gives us. This experience becomes our present to the world. It becomes the testimony that reminds other people that when they're going through hardships, when they're in their valleys and midnight hours, there is a God who cares about the intricate details of their lives. They need to be reminded that the One who created them knows them better than any human being will ever know them—and that He saved them and bought them with His Son's blood. When your heavenly Father says, "You're mine," He really means it!

To enjoy this transforming experience is our obligation. People want to take safe steps to achieve the big ideas God has given them; that's the human way. Everybody wants the path of least resistance on the way to fulfillment, the road to success that offers the smallest amount of pain. But I don't think there's a shortcut on this journey. You've got to go through all of it.

The true joy of the journey comes when you are stripped of who you are to become what you were created to be.

10: SERVICE

We had few operations in Asia in the early days; we were focused primarily on Africa and South America. Then the Indian Ocean tsunami hit on the day after Christmas in 2004.

A massive undersea earthquake that measured 9.3 on the Richter Scale killed over 300,000 people in coastal communities in over a dozen countries. Millions were left homeless and hopeless by this disaster, one of the worst the world has ever seen.

At the time, Kevin Donaldson, the president of Mission of Mercy, contacted me. His organization did a lot of work in Sri Lanka. Before the tsunami, the president of that country was telling any faith-based, Christian or humanitarian organizations that they had to leave the country. Mission of Mercy ran a series of orphanages in Sri Lanka, they had helped the government with consultation on establishing their welfare laws.

When the tsunami hit, Sri Lanka was one of the worst-affected countries—over 50,000 dead, and over a half million displaced. Tens of thousands of children were orphaned. The numbers were mind-boggling.

Kevin's organization was one of the few left that had an entrenched infrastructure in that nation, and now Sri Lanka was asking them to stay and help the country survive the aftermath. All of a sudden, this group was catapulted to a position of prominence in the nation. One of the things that they realized at the time was the urgent need for shoes. The physical landscape had been fundamentally altered—there were rocks sticking out everywhere, and the roads were too dangerous to travel on. These orphaned children had to walk barefoot along these treacherous roads.

Kevin and his partners asked us if we could help them with at least 20,000 pairs of shoes. We were able to route a supply to them, and we helped them give the shoes to children who needed them so badly. We trained their workers regarding how to do distributions. We also taught them how to get those shoes to the children quickly and efficiently, but without sacrificing the message of hope that went with them.

The response was phenomenal. Needs were met, children were blessed, and we were also able to provide other groups who were helping rebuild those ravaged countries with shoes to distribute.

At that moment in our history, we demonstrated our ability to mobilize and execute the game plan, and it really put Samaritan's Feet in the global spotlight. We had graduated to the big time. Because of this, our organization was connected with shoe companies that wanted to help us fulfill the needs of orphans from this devastating disaster.

Then, the following summer, Katrina hit. It was one disaster after another.

There was major, major devastation, and it was right here on our American home turf. Samaritan's Feet was ready, and we undertook that obligation to show the community love. We mobilized our networks, our partners, and churches everywhere. We had shoe drives all over the country. Then we took two truckloads of shoes down to New Orleans, and donated them to ministries.

Samaritan's Feet traveled to the Gulf three times in the weeks and months after Katrina. We helped rebuild homes, and we encouraged homeless people to not give up. We traveled to Mississippi cities such as Gulfport, where we sponsored a concert. We visited remote areas of Louisiana where everything was completely destroyed. We went to the New Orleans Superdome, where so many of the city's residents had sought refuge, and we offered them water to drink and food to eat.

I drove across Louisiana and Mississippi and saw the destitution this storm had ripped the cover off of. I didn't know there was such need in the Delta states, or that such hardship was even possible in this country. I saw abject poverty in stark relief under the magnifying glass of disaster, and it showed me that millions can lose it all with one misfortune. By the grace of God we are allowed to have what we have. Most of us are just one Katrina away from being one of those homeless people stumbling along the highway.

We were honored to give these people shoes. Our organization was able to distribute 20,000 pairs of shoes in the Gulf region in the wake of that tragedy.

Katrina leveled the playing field. One thing it taught me was that disaster knows no socioeconomic status, and definitely does not know color. It was so surreal to see white, black, Asians, Hispanics, all streaming into a huge football stadium. These people lost everything, and it didn't matter how much they had before the hurricane hit.

I couldn't figure out who the upper echelon of society had been, and I couldn't tell who the poorest bums who slept on the bridge were. These were all God's children who were suddenly in need, and the details didn't really matter.

An older white lady came up to me at our shoe distribution. "Thank you," she said. "The things that I take for granted... I never thought I would lose everything I had, or that my road back would lead me to a connection with a black person like you."

Perhaps this woman had never had a friendship or acquaintance with an African-American before, but she was crying, she was so filled with emotion. I knelt and prayed with her.

Our teams came to the Gulf region under the banner of love and compassion, and we were able to enter the properties of people that otherwise would have never interacted with African-American people in everyday life. We came to help them cut down half-fallen trees and clean up rubble, and to restore a sense of dignity and value to their land. Afterwards, we asked them if we could bless their households. They invited us inside their homes to pray with them.

We set up our tents and ministered to these people, and they all came to seek comfort. They were so grateful. I saw God's love modeled and demonstrated in a powerful way. "Thank you for coming," they said, looking into our eyes. "Thank you for blessing us."

Looking at those faces made me realize that in addition to the needs of the world, we also had to focus on domestic initiatives.

Several years before Katrina, Tracie and I attended a wedding in Blythesville, Arkansas. We flew out to Memphis and made the hour-long drive to Blythesville. We couldn't believe some of the communities we drove by. We saw people living in abandoned rail cars. There were no lights or indoor plumbing. There were ropes between trees where they hung their clothes to dry.

I thought we had been dropped into Haiti or rural Africa. "Is this really America?" I asked out loud.

In our overseas outreaches, I encountered a depth and level of poverty that transformed my spirit. As an organization, we had been doing all these great things internationally. Katrina brought us back home.

We found children without shoes in America! I was blown away. This wasn't supposed to happen here, this was a problem for other places. A long time ago, I used to think poor people only lived in third-world countries; did God ever prove me wrong!

Since the beginning of Samaritan's Feet, we've believed in the biblical model for missions. It's a very simple blueprint: when Christ gave His disciples a command to go out in the world, He said they would be His witnesses in Judea, Samaria, the outermost parts of the world. That model continues to this day, and we attempt to live up to it in places like Nigeria, Ecuador, and Sri Lanka, which are today's outermost parts of the world. We always knew that the greatest needs were overseas; when we first started, 95 percent of our projects were international.

The other five percent, here at home in the U.S., had mostly been work with our strategic partners to sponsor inner-city back-to-school shoe drives. But while Blythesville was my first encounter with the true depth of American poverty, I didn't act on my impulses to help until that hurricane hit. After Katrina, I realized we had to do more in the United States.

It was also apparent that to get to the next level we needed a major national campaign to help brand this Samaritan's Feet mission in the hearts and minds of the people in our own home country.

Todd Melloh was brought to Charlotte by Raycom Sports, where he worked in marketing. After he finished his contract for them, he was hired as the head of marketing for the local parks and recreation department for Mecklenburg County in North Carolina. That's how I first met Todd—we were organizing the Samaritan's Mile, our first barefoot 5K walk in 2004, and we reached out to his office.

I called him to see if Parks and Rec would partner with Samaritan's Feet to help this event happen. Memorial Stadium would be a great strategic downtown location, I told him—we could start and end the walk there and have a little celebration afterwards. There also was a water park, owned by the city and overseen by Todd, that regularly used its resources to help fund charitable activities in Charlotte. I wanted to see if they'd sponsor this walk.

When I spoke to Todd on the phone that day, I could hear in his voice that he was going through something. In our world, we often get so wrapped up in what we're trying to accomplish, so busy trying to get to the goal, that we forget what other people are going through on their journeys. For whatever reason, even though it was a busy day and we had all this business to tend to, God had me stop and ask Todd how we was doing. He wondered why I was asking.

"It just sounds like life is getting you down," I said. "It sounds like you're going through some major things. Can I meet with you just to chat?

He was taken aback by this stranger with his strange accent, delving into his personal life like that. But he agreed, and we met at a Chili's restaurant in Charlotte soon after. He was so grateful for the opportunity to pour his heart out to somebody, and he explained that it was a tough and transitional chapter of his life. He was going through a painful separation, and his children were coming to live with him. His estranged wife was seeing somebody else.

I stopped Todd and asked him, "Can I pray for you?" So we prayed there in that Chili's restaurant, and we ate together as he told me all of these things that were going on in his life. He secured a spot for our walk, set up the sponsor, but most importantly, a bond and a friendship had begun.

And it was all because I had left some room. Most of the time, we often don't leave enough margin for God. We forget that most of the miracles Christ performed were when His own agenda was interrupted. That day, God diverted my time schedule to focus on Todd's.

Todd and I started talking about matters beyond business, and became close friends. Eventually, Todd had to move back to Indianapolis because he lost custody of his children. We'd talk and pray together often over the phone, and I'd try to encourage him.

My life wasn't easy at that time either. These were the early days of Samaritan's Feet, when our family finances were in ruins, when I wondered when God was going to show up.

One of the ways He did was through a software company in Wisconsin called RedPrairie that brought me on to manage its product group. Between 2004 and 2005, I would spend Monday through Thursday in Waukesha, helping run this company's product group. RedPrairie was, at the time, a 60 million dollar company that had just bought a 40 million dollar software firm from the United Kingdom, so it had become a 100 million dollar behemoth. In addition to all that, they were trying to migrate their offshore development from India to China.

For the first time in my life, I had a conflicting objective! I was helping to run this giant software company's product group, and at the same time was managing this worldwide ministry called Samaritan's Feet to fulfill my God-given mandate to touch the world. But I needed money to keep the mission going, and the executives at RedPrairie were willing to let me focus on giving shoes as long as I was able to take care of the business side too.

The chief operating officer believed in what I was doing, and told me, "Manny, you go do what God's called you to do. Just make sure you deliver what we've brought you here to do."

So every evening while I was in Wisconsin, Todd and I would chat. He was going through a series of job situations in which he felt painfully unfulfilled. He worked for public relations companies and marketing firms, but he felt an itch I was all too familiar with.

"I know I'm called to do something," Todd told me.

"Come work for us," I offered. "Just one thing, though. I don't have money to pay you."

Todd was remarrying, and he couldn't work for free.

"Hey, buddy, if you know this is what God has called you to do, come join us!" I said. "We'll make a way."

Over the following year, RedPrairie realized that my passion and desire lay elsewhere, and let me off the hook. But they ended up taking care of me for six extra months, and RedPrairie remains a major supporter of Samaritan's Feet to this day. In 2009, the firm committed to providing us with the logistics software that will streamline our supply-chain processes. This is how much RedPrairie believes in our cause.

Meanwhile, Todd was trying to satisfy his call to action. He tried applying at every major ministry in Indianapolis, but because of his history as a divorcée, very few Christian organizations would hire him. They always had one reason or another for rejecting him. He was hungry to use his gifts as a marketer to influence and impact God's kingdom, yet nobody would give him a chance.

"What is it going to take for me to come work for you?" Todd asked me in 2007. "I know that God wants me to help you somehow, Manny. I am dying in these jobs, nobody will give me an opportunity in the ministry. But I need to get out and serve. Offer me a salary. I'll take anything."

Things were much better for Samaritan's Feet by then, but I had little to offer him financially. I gave him a number, one that was a mere fraction of what he was making in the marketing business.

Todd accepted.

His contracted responsibility was to work with a public relations firm and spearhead our efforts to get the Samaritan's Feet name out to the American public. We were successful internationally, and we had made a real impact during the Indian Ocean tsunami, but we were still fighting for name recognition in our own homeland. The more people knew about us here, we figured, the more people would be mobilized to help us achieve our mission of 10 million pairs of shoes for 10 million children in 10 years. So Todd got to work establishing our brand in the United States.

One of Todd's first initiatives was to team up with Thomas Kinkade, the "Painter of Light," and we forged an agreement for him to donate the proceeds from prints of his painting of the 2007 Rockefeller Plaza

Christmas tree lighting.

We went to New York, but things didn't turn out the way we envisioned. But the secondary reason why we were there was the opportunity to meet Dr. Maya Angelou at a Gabarron Foundation function, where she was receiving a lifetime achievement award.

But God certainly flipped that script! He was taking us to New York for an entirely different reason.

Dr. Angelou inspired us so much that we went into that hotel room at the New Yorker, where Todd came up with the vision for barefoot coaching. It was Todd's idea to have a Division I head coach walk the sidelines in his bare feet, and it was Todd's idea to call up Ron Hunter of IUPUI late at night.

Recently, the Governor of West Virginia went barefoot for a day, and Todd and I went to that state in order to attend the ceremony. It was there Told me, "Manny, I used to think that I went to Charlotte to work for Raycom. At that time in my life, I felt like a failure at everything. I didn't realize that God brought me to Charlotte after all the things I went through to meet you, and to put me in that hotel room in New York at that particular moment."

Todd's vision wasn't only a good idea, it was a God idea too. We never talked about doing any barefoot stuff before that time. In that hotel room, we asked ourselves, What do we do? The answer was simple: we put shoes on kids' feet. And once we said "Yes" to help provide shoes for children, it opened the door to deliver many other types of help as well.

When Samaritan's Feet opened an office on the west coast, the volunteers out there quickly encountered a level of need beyond belief. Most of that need was in the inner cities, places like Compton and San Bernardino and Long Beach. With the help of one of our board members, we opened an office in Washington, D.C., to start an inner-city ministry.

The D.C. office offered some very powerful opportunities for us. Ballou High School is one of the more famous high schools in the southeastern section of Washington; it's known for outstanding sports programs that have produced many great athletes. But Ballou is in a community that's been ravaged with gang violence. There's a bridge nearby that connects the neighborhood with the upscale area where the Nationals baseball team plays. But once you cross that bridge, you've entered a place where nobody wants to be. It was rumored that the police ignore what goes on in that community, that they'd just given up on the people who live there.

We heard a tragic story about a woman in that neighborhood who killed her children. The only reason why anybody found that out was because the landlord was getting ready to serve an eviction notice. She was sitting there in front of her house when the sheriff arrived with the papers, and the stench from the rotting bodies alerted the sheriff that something was terribly wrong.

The police didn't even know those kids were missing, much less dead. There were stories in the news later that told how people in the community had tried to contact the cops, to let them know about this horrible stench that was taking over the neighborhood. Some said the police had simply ignored all those reports. This was a completely forgotten area of the nation's capital, right under the noses of the President, Congress, and the Supreme Court.

When our regional coordinator contacted me and told me of this story, I fired back, "We've got to get in there."

Samaritan's Feet initially planned to reach 1,000 children in that community, but we wanted to make sure that we were creating bridges. We connected with community leadership, the police, multiple churches, and crossed denominational lines to bring people together. We were focused on making progress on the issues these forgotten residents faced.

For our first shoe distribution there, we had the police and the health department working together with community leaders. We planned children's programs, had festival activities, and promoted an atmosphere of joy. In a gesture that had never been seen before in the history of D.C., Mayor Fenty granted Samaritan's Feet permission to close a street, and we were empowered to direct the police in terms of what we needed to do in that community. (It was a miracle by itself to get that paperwork for the clearances to be filed properly, considering the speed that all of this came together.) We had the police officers knock on the doors of people's homes and told parents to bring their kids to receive a free pair of shoes.

We learned that a truce was drawn by rival gangs on that day. Gang members had been shooting each other so often that nobody walked the streets in that area, but people came out of their homes in broad daylight to participate in fellowship with us.

It was powerful to see all the battle lines disappear. It was a picture of mini-heaven! We saw whites kneeling on the ground serving blacks by washing their feet, we saw blacks returning the favor to whites. The police chief came and washed the feet of children.

When some of the gang members saw all this, they were really taken aback.

We found out later that the effects of that day were long-lasting. The following Sunday, some gang members came to the local church and offered to turn in their guns for Bibles. "We saw the leaders of this community stand up," one of them said. "We saw the police chief wash the feet of our poor kids, and we want to know more about the God who inspired that."

We've gone back to that community twice since then. We have provided shoes for the Ballou football and basketball teams. We've been able to supply resources to that school full of disadvantaged kids, and it's been a phenomenal opportunity. Coach Moses Ware became the first high school football coach to go barefoot for us during a game. The Washington media covered the event, bringing more awareness to our cause domestically.

We partnered with the NCAA and ran an event at the 2009 Final Four in Detroit. At first, they weren't so sure about all this foot-washing business. This wasn't really the image they wanted to put across. For a long time, we could not get an audience at the senior level of the NCAA, we were unable to get them to seriously consider partnering with us for an event. But the coaches, as well as the local organizing committee, called the top dogs at the NCAA and got us in the door! Lowe's donated basketball hoop kits and we were going to have coaches washing feet. It had the potential be a great event that would touch many lives.

The day came, and we showed up at the Coleman Young Center in the morning along with several trucks, and set about preparing to bless 1,000 inner-city kids. Clark Kellogg, the CBS basketball analyst, showed up too.

"I've heard what you do," he said to me when we were introduced. "You guys are for real. I just want to see this for myself."

Clark was for real too, he wasn't just there for a photo opportunity. He was there to serve, and he got down in the trenches with the 100 or so Detroit-area volunteers. He helped us sort the shoes for the day's distribution, and set up washing stations. After we finished setting up, he was so moved to see the scope and the size of what we were doing.

"You're going to wash all those kids' feet?" he asked me.

"Absolutely," I replied.

He had to go do a television show that morning, but he asked me, "Can I come back around five o'clock?"

At five on the dot, Clark returned. At that time, the shoe distribution had begun, and more than 20 college basketball coaches had arrived to roll up their sleeves and get to work. Kids were there who had been bused in from children's homes and homeless shelters all around Detroit. The city is severely economically depressed with so many lost jobs, the amount of need was incredible. When those kids came off the buses, they couldn't believe this was really happening. Nobody had ever seen anything like what we were doing.

Clark and the coaches were down on their knees touching and blessing those kids. The wives of the coaches were also getting involved, and the volunteers were all working hard to reach these children with new shoes and a message of hope. I remember one teenage boy who came up to me after South Dakota State head coach Scott Nagy had washed his feet. He was wearing his brand new Nike basketball shoes, and he gave me a big hug.

"I've been living in a foster home all my life," he told me as tears started welling up in his eyes. "I've never seen anything new before. Ever."

He had his old shoes with him, and they were dirty and raggedy with holes in them. They were falling apart. But to my surprise, he held them in front of him, offering them to me. "Is it okay if I give you my old shoes? I know somebody needs them. I want to pass them on."

"No, no, man, it's okay," I said, waving him off. Those shoes stunk! I had to literally force him to throw them away. But that kid was so selfless and generous, he wanted to make sure his shoes went to someone else. How I wish I'd taken those shoes and framed them as a constant reminder of this memorable day.

Afterwards, I was talking to the director of that boy's foster home. "You don't know what you did for that kid, the one who tried to give you back his shoes," he told me. I responded, "It was nothing, man, we do this all the time."

"No, no, you don't understand. That kid normally won't say a word, he lives in a shell. He says nothing to anybody. You guys cracked the veneer and broke him."

In 2006, a new middle school in Charlotte was opened called the Martin Luther King, Jr. School. Considering the leader this man was, it seems like every time they name a street, building, or a school after Dr. King, it's always in an impoverished neighborhood. This school was brand new and was tucked away in a poor area called Hidden Valley, on Charlotte's east side.

When MLK opened up, it proved to be a real challenge to school leadership. There were a lot of gang-related problems, single-parent households, and drugs. Every inner-city issue you can think of was stacking the deck against this new school. I found out from Mark Robertson, the principal, that in the first year a huge percentage of these seventh-graders were suspended because of truancy, fights, and all sorts of other problems. The students had no respect whatsoever for the teachers, and it was an atmosphere of mutual mistrust. Mark was searching for answers as to how to turn things around.

At that time, I was serving on the board of an inner-city ministry called Urban Restoration. Much of what we were doing was trying to reach into and make a difference in the Hidden Valley neighborhood. Colin Pinkney, UR's executive director, put together a coalition that included Cary Mitchell (a designer of custom clothes for NBA players), myself, and a local photographer and businessman named Michael Valentine.

Michael had the vision to create Xtreeme Challenge, a team-building ropes course facility south of Charlotte, where he would bring at-risk kids to the countryside. This was a place to get them away from their familiar surroundings, and pair them together with their peers and teachers to build trust. Most of these kids had never been out of the city before. They'd go through these high ropes, and they would be 10 or 20 feet above ground. Everybody would need each other's help to complete these tasks.

Debbie Kaclick was the athletic director at MLK School at that time, and she had a heart for her pupils. She worked with us to figure out ways to bus different classes to Xtreeme Challenge every Friday. We had peer groups and mentors work with those kids in neutral surroundings, and put them through the ropes course. While they were out there, Debbie and these groups would talk about life with them, encourage and inspire them. The whole idea was to build bridges between the students and the teachers, and in the course of a couple of months, every child in that school had gone through this process.

I was out there visiting one Friday and remember seeing one of the teachers having a lot of trouble with the students. They were so disrespectful, talking back and using the worst kind of language. I was horrified. "I wish this was in Africa," I said. "No child talks that way to an adult over there. I wish I had the opportunity to transport these kids to that continent for two weeks and immerse them in African life."

That's when the idea and inspiration for the Samaritan's Feet Youth Ambassador Program percolated in my mind. I wanted to figure out some way to make them realize that even though they maybe poor in this country, they're some of the wealthiest people in the world. They have no excuses for the way they act. I wanted these students to sit in African classrooms with kids their age, wash the feet of the poor kids, and learn to serve. One thing that these kids clearly didn't know how to do was serve; they thought they were placed on earth to be served.

I imagined some type of scholarship or grant process that would get them to apply to go to Africa. The longer I thought about this, it became more and more real. I shared this idea with Colin, Debbie and Mark.

"That would be phenomenal, Manny," Mark the principal said. "These kids need to see another part of the world and get some perspective. Most of them have never been out of Mecklenburg County. Being on a 15-hour flight across the Atlantic Ocean to Africa... that alone would change their lives."

We put together a plan, and I asked local businessmen like Michael and Cary if they would fund an initiative like this. They decided to partner with us and raise grant money for a pilot program in 2007, sponsoring students and ten chaperones to come with Samaritan's Feet to Africa. The requirement for those applicants was an essay, "Why I Want to Be a Youth Ambassador." There were 12 community leaders who judged the entries, and each of the finalists had to come before the board and defend their reasoning. Each also had to maintain a B average in school and put in at least 30 hours of community service. The selection process was rigorous, and we stressed parental involvement.

We tried to blend inner-city students with those from wealthy neighborhoods, so we could have at-risk children alongside upper-middle-class kids from higher achievement schools, so that they would all learn from the dynamics. We blended African-American, Caucasian and Hispanic students.

When we touched down in Africa, the effects were stunning.

The transformations were unbelievable—physically, educationally, culturally, and spiritually. All the walls just crumbled. Cultural barriers we erect in the United States were demolished. Spiritual barriers based on denominations were knocked down. Economic barriers were smashed. These kids broke through all the things that hold them back, and gelled as an army of one.

They got up early in the morning and went into classrooms with their chaperones, and they were shocked to see that sixth graders over there were learning what we'd consider to be eighth grade math! They went to the orphanages and soup kitchens, they were involved in shoe distributions, and our team ended up touching the lives of over 2,000 people on that trip.

I saw how some of the young ladies on the trip were changed. Several weren't comfortable speaking in public when they arrived in Africa. But they had to stand in front of 2,000 students and share the reasons why they were there. By the time they came back to America, they were doing interviews on national television! The principals couldn't believe what had happened with these kids.

As part of their assignment, YAP kids have to build a model of a non-profit organization when they return to America. One of our recent YAP projects was to outfit an entire primary school in rural South Africa with uniforms. Many of those students have tattered clothes and are unable to protect themselves from the winter cold.

Our young team raised the funds by designing a t-shirt that they marketed and sold, then used the proceeds to purchase uniforms for every student at the school in that farming community.

The Youth Ambassador Program continues to grow. In its second year, we took children from four different schools in the Charlotte area. In 2009, we took kids from eight schools. We are now planning to bring students from eight schools to White River, South Africa, the community of orphan-headed households that so touched Dr. Ski.

I see this as a vehicle and a framework to help mold young people and turn their focus away from themselves and towards the world. YAP teaches them that they are blessed, and that they have a responsibility to bless others.

If we can engage these lives at a young age, if we can let them see themselves as conduits to make this world a better place, I truly believe that this will shape the future of those kids as they go through high school, college, and the business world. They will remember to be philanthropists for the rest of their lives, and leave behind lasting legacies.

There's a young man named Tajir. He was in seventh grade when he went with us to Africa as part of the first YAP program. He was a gifted athlete, playing football and running track. After he came back, his grades shot through the roof and he became one of the most disciplined young men I've ever met. "Mr, Manny, I know I'm a great athlete and I know I'll probably be a great businessman someday," he told me. "But I believe that I was called to be a minister after I came back from that trip."

Tajir's mother said that his work ethic, focus, dedication, and commitment were so different when he returned. That Christmas, his mother called me and told me about a conversation they'd had.

"Mom, I don't want any gifts this Christmas," her son said. "Mom, there are people out there with real needs. I saw the poverty of Africa, and

175

I know I don't need another toy or game or piece of clothing. I have enough."

She told me that's when she knew that YAP had changed her son's life forever. He had been transformed from self-centered to selfless.

In 2008, we saw our percentage of domestic initiatives rise to represent 40 percent of our total projects. The volume of shoes is still greater internationally, because we send containers overseas and work with local indigenous peoples to maximize the impact. But the number of projects we do here in the United States will soon represent over half of our outreach.

The response has been incredible and it's thrilling to see the growth. Much of this has to do with the economy and where we are as a nation, as more and more parents struggle to decide between buying groceries and putting shoes on the feet of their children. We're able to help meet those needs, which then leads to other opportunities to minister to them.

Some Americans were fortunate to come from high net-worth families, but the majority of our middle class come from humble beginnings and immigrant stock. Almost every American that I've ever spoken to can still remember what it was like to receive their first pair of brand-new shoes. That image is burned into their mind, it was like Christmas. So when you tell them that there are young adults in this country who are 15, 16, 17 years old who have never had a pair of new shoes in their lives, they say, "What?!" They simply can't believe it.

Recently in Greensboro, North Carolina, we met a young girl whose parents were homeless and she had no shoes.

When you think of the health implications of foot-borne diseases, if you can grasp the concept of thousands of shoeless children right here in America, you can also realize that each individual can actually do something about it. Each contribution of a pair of shoes makes a direct impact. You know that pair of shoes is going to a person they will really help.

We tell parents to go shopping with their sons or daughters. Buy a pair of shoes in their size, we tell them. Use that transaction as a life-lesson opportunity. There's a child in a poor community here in America, or somewhere overseas, who has the same size shoe as your son or daughter. Your child can write a note to that kid, a short letter of hope and encouragement. That simple act will help them feel they're connected. They are making a true difference in the life of somebody somewhere who may not be able to afford a pair of shoes, but is the same age and shoe size as them.

NUGGETS OF VIRTUE

The biggest excuse I hear in churches today is this: "We don't have the resources to serve." That's something we as individuals also say a lot. There are all sorts of excuses we make for not doing all we can. But God's called us to do something... and that means *all* of us. You have to participate in the process; the spiritual life is not a spectator sport, and you must get in the game. It's not about what you know, it's about what you do. The one who loves is the one who gets involved; the one who loves is the one who gives not only what they *have*, but also what they *are*.

There is a Hispanic church here in Charlotte with only 40 members. Most of them were immigrants, and some are undocumented. Many don't have jobs or money. But they have a heart to minister to the poor of their community. They were looking for an opportunity to serve, and they connected with Samaritan's Feet.

But we told them, "We don't just want to give you the shoes, we want to give you the opportunity to help raise the resources to make this possible. Then you will own a part of this vision, because you are blessed when you bless others."

This 40-member church couldn't afford to buy the 200 pairs of shoes for this distribution, but they also couldn't afford not to. The congregation realized that they were called to serve the needy of the community in Matthew 25:40, "As you have done unto the least of my brethren, you have done it unto me." So church members would each pick up change on the ground or pennies from their pockets, keep it in jars at home and bring it in on Sunday. There was a wheelbarrow they used for the weekly collection and people would drop their change in. And within six weeks, those poor families had enough to fund a 200-person distribution in Charlotte. The project was called "Pick Up a Penny."

At first, that congregation didn't have the resources, and they didn't believe they could complete the task. But we told them to dream beyond themselves. When they had accomplished their goal, you should have seen their joy. They thought they were poor, but had worked together to help people in the community even poorer than they were! They were so proud to be a part of the economy of God's blessings.

You might think you have nothing to give to God. But ask yourself, "What do I have in my hand?" The Lord always accepts anything you have at your disposal, no matter how big or small.

Somebody once told me that the greatest gift that we can give is one that costs nothing: it is our smile. It might sound corny at face value, but there's an entire ministry inside that statement. People always talk about the things that they can't do, citing the high cost of doing good. But let me tell you about the greatest no-cost gift there is: the joy, the smile on your face. Whatever life presents us, good or bad, we can always choose to be joyful, and nobody can ever take that choice away from us.

Happiness is a state of mind, but joy is something that can transcend feelings and circumstances. When you pour yourself into something that's bigger than you, when you answer the command of God to serve humanity and give back, I believe that "Yes" diminishes whatever your problems are. You turn your attention to the plight of others and can put things into proper perspective. You realize that you are blessed and that you have a reason to be joyful.

I feel that I am an open channel and a window in God's eyes, one that can be used to fulfill a key aspect of what the Lord is trying to do in this world. To convey this message, He uses vessels who are willing to participate in the process of taking part in what He has designed.

He's looking for people who are willing to lay down their own selfish desires, their wants and their needs, and make themselves His representatives. Once we align ourselves with Him, when we allow our will to be linked with His, then God takes our focus and our faithfulness and transforms them into ministry. That service, in turn, changes the world.

A friend of mine told me recently, "God sees our tears, but He's not really moved by them. He's moved by our faithfulness." He honors our commitment because He knows the price we've paid for choosing to say Yes. Obedience is one of the most expensive virtues. God knows the cost. He saw His Son pay the bill for all humanity two millenniums ago.

If we are willing to follow Christ's example and pay the price of obedience, God will reward us with all the resources we need with which to serve Him.

11: FAMILY

I was originally supposed to be the shoe man, now they call me the "sole man." This is because I completed a 300-mile barefoot walk from Charlotte to Atlanta in October 2008. I walked through one town and heard somebody yell out, "Here comes the sole man!"

Of all the things I've ever accomplished, the World Walk was the toughest, most gruesome and the most painful, but also the most loving —all wrapped up in a single two-week experience. It was definitely the most daring thing I've ever done so far. For somebody to say that he wants to walk 300 miles in his bare feet, that brother had better be crazy or close to it! But I wanted to put my feet in line with what my mouth was professing. Samaritan's Feet is telling the world that 300 million children don't have shoes, and I felt it was time to take my own shoes off and walk my talk.

I've seen the reality of shoelessness with my own eyes, over and over again, all around the world. But that 300-mile walk gave me a whole new depth of passion for what Samaritan's Feet does. Now I can speak about what those children are going through from personal experience. I grew up poor and humble in Nigeria myself, but I'd been in the United States for 20 years. I forgot what it was like to not have shoes... my feet got Americanized!

Because I said "Yes" to this undertaking, God brought the NASCAR community with us. My friend Marcus Smith with Speedway Motorsports said "Yes" too, and opened his track, the Lowe's Motor Speedway, to allow us to hold a first-of-its-kind "Barefoot Breakfast." People within the sports, business, and church communities united together to learn about our vision. There were many celebrities there, NFL players, NBA players, and NASCAR drivers.

Thanks to Marcus saying Yes, the owners of JTG Racing approached us and said that they wanted to donate temporary sponsorship on a race car. This was one of the coolest Yes'es I've ever seen! It was the No. 47 race car in the Nationwide Series; it had our World Walk logo on the hood, with footprints going up and down the sides of the automobile. It finished seventh in the Saturday race that weekend, and we got to watch trackside. To see that car with "Samaritan's Feet World Walk" on it racing around that oval... *wow!*

I was originally going to walk the 600 or so miles from Charlotte to New York City. That distance scared me off, because it looked like it was going to take me a lifetime! Atlanta didn't seem that far away by comparison, and it would take two weeks. I consoled myself that it only takes an hour to fly between the two cities.

Seriously, how hard could it be to walk that far?

After the first day, I realized that I'd been gone from Africa for a long, long time. My feet started talking to me!

"Brother, was this your idea?" they were saying. "Who gave you permission to punish us like this? We weren't invited to that strategy session! Put us back in those shoes this instant!"

I wore those feet out. We walked 24 miles the first day, then 27 the next, then another 25 on the third day... and let me tell you, that third day was the longest day of my life. There were so many hills around Blacksburg, South Carolina, and it was really hot (around 85 degrees), so it felt like someone was cooking my feet in a skillet!

Even though I had worked out with a wonderful trainer named Calvin Fleming and prepared as best I could, I was breaking down. Nothing could truly prepare me for the actual task except the journey itself. The cracks in the road are the last thing on your mind when you're driving along at 65 miles per hour, but when your feet are up against that asphalt, pain is going to find you one way or another.

After the first few days, I felt like this World Walk was going to take me a month to complete. I didn't go to South Africa with my wife and a team of our Youth Ambassador Program members that fall, because I needed at least four weeks to recover from the pounding my feet took! Everywhere I stopped, a podiatrist examined my feet and applied iodine and antibiotics to them. I had blisters like crazy. I lost a couple of toenails because I hit them against rocks. At the end of every day, my feet were swollen. You'd have thought I was pregnant or something!

Creativity comes out of nowhere, but it really shows up when you're trying to avoid suffering. I learned that walking on top of the white lines provided some temporary comfort. And I discovered there are different grades of gravel when you go from one county to the next. You can learn a lot about how much is in a county's transportation budget from their roads! There were some places where the rocks were so big and coarse, I could tell that they hadn't ordered the top quality gravel, the kind that's been ground up a few extra times.

"Oh, nobody ever walks through this part of town," I'm sure they were saying. They didn't know Manny was going to come by one day, in his bare feet no less!

When someone needs medical attention in America, there are a million hospitals, urgent care centers, emergency rooms, and there's always a Walgreen's, Rite Aid, or CVS somewhere nearby. In countries like Nigeria, Guyana, and Brazil, where children walk across broken glass and stones because they can't afford shoes, there's none of that. They pray.

Their hospital is their closet, where they ask God if He will perform a miracle and cure maladies as minor as a simple cut. An aspirin or a Band-Aid isn't readily available to them. Basic, small, preventable ailments cause people to lose their lives. God is their only doctor.

At the end of each day, my team would pray for me. And every morning, it was as if God regenerated my soles and gave me a new pair of feet. It was the weirdest, yet most profound feeling. I would start every day fresh, and walk over 20 miles as if it was nothing. When the journey was painful, God helped me focus on people other than myself. He used that time every day to center my attention on those children, and that chased the pain away.

Images played in my mind. I saw the faces of those mothers in Guyana who showed up at 5 o'clock in the morning so they could be the first ones in line to get a pair of shoes for their children. I remembered all the times we'd run out of shoes, and there were still a couple thousand more people out there waiting. The need is so much greater than the resources, so much more than one person can fulfill. I just wanted more people to know about the need, so they could join me on this crusade. That's why I was walking.

Each time I stepped on a rock or some sharp object, I would yell out the name of a child. I would call out names like Hafeez, Pedro, Sunday, Albert, Julio, and Jai.

In my own pain, I would shout out their names and pray for them. I prayed that God would remember their sufferings. I stepped on plenty of sharp objects on those roads, but I never ran out of names.

Many people embraced us on our journey. They saw that we were doing something for a bigger cause, that this was not for our personal ego. We were drawing attention to the plight of others less fortunate, and that was the primary reason we were putting ourselves through this gruesome punishment.

I'd never felt so much love from strangers, even through the South Carolina back country, where there have long been severely-drawn racial dividing lines. There were some stores along the road, and I was likely the first African-American to ever set foot in them.

Through the whole two-week walk, we had an advance team go ahead of us. There was only one town where we had to make alternate plans. Our representative went and talked to the local sheriff, and he informed us, "I know this man's a nice guy and he's doing a great thing, but if you really love him I'd reroute him around this community. There are some folks who don't like his particular skin color around here."

But that was the only exception. Everywhere else, none of that mattered. White, black, Hispanic, I hugged and loved on everybody that we met. They hugged me back, and some gave me high fives as I walked by. I went to schools and inspired young kids to dream. Damien Horne, a Nashville-based recording artist, played mini-concerts every day. I stopped by churches and shared my testimony and message of hope.

"Regardless of what's in your past, follow your dreams into the future," I told people along the way. "Let me tell you about the One who can unlock your tomorrows, and heal your yesterdays."

One of the stories I'll never forget happened right outside of Anderson, South Carolina. I was making my way through some back hills, and most people don't walk through that part of the country. And with our entourage, we were quite a sight! We had two RV's, the No. 47 race car, and this African brother leading the way. At any given time we'd have 12 to 20 other people walking with us. As we approached, one of our representatives would be walking along, giving out brochures and answering the inevitable questions: *what* is this spectacle, and *why*?

"We're walking on behalf of 300 million kids around the world who don't have shoes," our volunteers would tell them. "That's why Manny's walking from Charlotte to Atlanta in his bare feet, to draw attention to this immense need."

In Anderson, there was a woman and her daughter who were sitting in front of their house, watching us walk by. They must have been thinking, Who in the heck are these people? Then when one of our volunteers gave the lady a brochure and explained Samaritan's Feet to her, she asked, "Can you guys hold on one minute?"

She walked gingerly back into her house. Her daughter (whose name was Rosie) said, "It's so commendable what you're doing. My mother just suffered a stroke, she's retired and on Social Security. She knows no stranger, never has known one in her whole life."

Rosie's mother came back outside, and she was holding a five-dollar bill in her hand. "Do you think this can help?" she asked with slurred speech, a result of her stroke. "Will this help out to provide shoes to kids?"

I told her it would, as my eyes moistened.

"I'm on Social Security, and this is the last money I have this month," she explained regretfully. "Please give this to those children, and tell them that somebody here in South Carolina is praying for them."

Through my tears, I asked her if I could pray for her.

"No, no, no," she responded. "Can I pray for *you*?"

It was as if God sent that lady to put fuel in my engine. I was tired, ready for the day's journey to be over. But this encounter put wind in my sail, it was a meeting sealed in heaven. That woman had a widow's mite, and gave the last pennies she had so that somebody else could be blessed. We prayed together and I told her, "Pray for me, and pray for the millions of children around the world."

We had young kids, elementary school students, walk with me. When I walked past Emmanuel College in Georgia, over 100 students got up and walked with us for four or five miles. People all along the way were inspired to donate shoes or offer money for our effort.

Then, two weeks after I first set out, we arrived in Atlanta. When I saw the city limits sign up ahead, I yelled out, "Lord have mercy! I'm finally here!"

We made our way to a local Bass Pro Shop, and Ernie Johnson from "Inside the NBA" on TNT met us there with his family. People from the Atlanta community came and took off their shoes to walk the final mile with me. It was powerful to see that ocean of bare feet streaming towards the Atlanta Motor Speedway.

Since the World Walk, I've been able to speak to this cause from first-hand experience. I only suffered for two weeks, but those 300 million children walk without shoes every single day.

The head of Crocs' humanitarian efforts, Melissa Koester, walked with me for four days. She was blown away, she couldn't believe that these Samaritan's Feet people were putting action behind their words. We were putting our money where our mouths were! After a mile or two, she took off her comfortable shoes too and walked barefoot alongside me. After the World Walk, Crocs felt compelled to donate over a million pairs of shoes to be delivered over the following four years.

You have a lot of thinking time on your hands when you walk for nine hours a day.

My mind went back to when I was a small child in Nigeria. I thought about my mother, how she sacrificed everything she had so her son could fulfill his dream. Growing up, my mom always told me that I would one day serve God. I always told my mom I wanted to make *money*, that's what *I* wanted to do. My father wanted me to be a doctor, but God had a different plan.

As you have already read, I was blessed to have the opportunity to earn a basketball scholarship and come to America, to get my undergraduate degree and my Master's, and then to become a success in the business world.

I thought about my relationship with my father and played a lot of tapes in my head of those painful interactions. I thought about the horrible and damaging effect alcohol had on his life, how he became a different person when he drank. I remembered how he used to say that I'd never amount to much. In the most defining time of my childhood, when I was becoming a man, my father wasn't there for me. I reflected on his good heart, his poor decisions, and all the time we missed together. But I celebrated the fact that I'll see him in heaven, because he came to know Christ before he passed away.

My family walked with me. When my flesh wanted to give in, when my muscles wanted to shut down, they were there to encourage me. When I was tired they reminded me why I was doing this. "We're almost there, daddy," my children kept telling me, "We're so proud of you."

Their support meant the world to me. Each of them walked barefoot at some point of the journey, to empathize and feel what those 300 million children of God around the world go through every day. They can say they've been there and can understand what it is to go without shoes, because they took off their own and walked with their father for many miles.

There was so much time for introspection while on the road. I walked through that rugged terrain in the back country, those valleys and peaks, miles of grass and dandelions and cow pastures that I passed by—the beauty of God's creation. I thought about my family, the dreams I have for them. I reflected daily on how real and pure Tracie's love is for me and our children. She juggles so many roles as a wife, an executive at Samaritan's Feet who's in charge of our finances, as a principal and teacher for home-schooled students, a leader and a friend in the community. Wonder Woman has absolutely nothing on my wonderful wife!

And I thought about our children, the promise that their futures hold.

Nike (pronounced nee-KAY), my oldest daughter, was born on January 15, 1994 at the Dakota Clinic in Fargo. It was one of the coldest of all the frigid days in North Dakota. People didn't know Tracie was pregnant for a long time, because she was very tall and skinny as a stick. And she had the longest labor. The whole process was excruciating for both of us—for her more so than for me, of course.

We didn't know we were having a girl, because we didn't want to have an ultrasound. We wanted God to surprise us. And I was surprised! She came out looking just like me. I remember putting that little baby in the car and driving her home to our apartment. During the car ride I truly realized I'd crossed over a wide chasm. I was no longer just Manny, we were no longer Manny and Tracie... now there was somebody else who bore my name and DNA, and I embraced the challenge of a child. What a joyful day that was. I held Nike so much when she was tiny.

To this day, she favors her daddy. Nike reminds me so much of myself, she's like a mirror image of me. She has the same outgoing personality, she loves people, and she's a tomboy athlete who plays basketball and volleyball. Her dream is to open a sports academy in South Africa. I've always known that she's destined to do great things in this world.

Tracie and I just loved being parents, so we planned to have another child. And God blessed us with another beautiful girl on July 24, 1996 after we'd moved to North Carolina.

Dele (pronounced deh-LEH) reminds me so much of Tracie. I protect Dele so much, because she makes me think of my bride. Growing up, whenever they'd get in trouble at school, I'd always take Dele's side and Tracie would always take Nike's side. In my eyes, Dele couldn't do anything wrong! She always got a little extra leeway.

Dele was such a contented baby, while Nike always needed TLC growing up. We could hardly eat at a restaurant. We'd go to the Olive Garden, and on cue, when our food came Nike would start *screaming*. It would get so bad that we'd have to leave! We'd have to rock and console her... but Dele was the complete opposite. Dele has always carried herself with such grace, like she was a princess or a queen. Nike will go out for all the teams, but Dele doesn't want to mess with any of that stuff. She's more interested in acting, modeling, art, and photography. "Please don't make me do any sports, dad," she always says.

"As long as you live under my roof, you're going to play sports," I always tell Dele. "Once you graduate, you can do whatever you want!"

So Dele plays some basketball too. She's smart. Things come easy to her and she's always in a different category than her peers. She's very mature for her age, and wants to be a pediatrician, and I know she's going to be successful at anything she puts her mind to.

All of our children have African names. Because we carry these names through life from birth to death, I believe that names must have meaning. My name, Emmanuel, is: "God is with us." My oldest daughter is Adenike, which means "the worth of my princess' crown has been preserved." My second daughter's name is Oladele, which means "success has come home."

Our third daughter's name is Oluyemisi, meaning "God provided her to bless us." Yemi was born in 1999, at a very busy and transitional period of our lives. It was an incredible time of financial success for us, in the middle of a very difficult year. I was wrapping up my obligations in New York and was getting ready to transition back to Charlotte. I was always traveling, everything was moving so fast in my life.

Yemi (pronounced YEM-ee) is one of the best self-starters and self-learners I know. She taught herself how to swim, and she was the fastest of our children to learn how to ride a bike. I held her only twice, then she was off and going. She taught herself how to tie her shoes. Everything that moms and dads have to teach kids, she was way ahead of our game! She's a tech wizard, she loves basketball, and she adores animals. She's already made up her mind that she wants to be a veterinarian. If it were up to Yemi, our house would be a full-blown zoo!

After our third daughter was born, I got on my knees and said, "God, you know I'm an African. Please bless me with the seed to carry my name and legacy forward."

Tracie told me I had one more shot at a son or I was going to have to close up the shop. So after we conceived for a fourth time, I made that call to Dr. Watson to set up an appointment for a vasectomy. I remember talking to my male friends in Nigeria about it. They would say, "Is this some kind of American thing? Are you crazy? We don't do that here in Africa!"

I changed my appointment five or six times until I ran out of excuses.

I had to keep the Ohonme name alive for another generation, so I was praying to the Lord for a miracle! On February 4, 2002, in the year before we started Samaritan's Feet, Adewale was born.

Praise God, a son! The name we gave him means "the king has come home."

I was so excited when God blessed us with Wale. The community we live in is very international, we have Indian families living on both sides of our house. Wale's best friends are these kids from India, and all their parents love him dearly. He's like the king of the mafia in our community, whenever somebody's been treated wrong, Wale will come to their defense. He has such a big heart, and he treats all his friends like gold.

Wale (pronounced WALL-eh) has been such a joy to Tracie and I, so full of life, strength, and vigor. He's a natural athlete. I really believe that he will do dynamic things with his life. I just pray that he always keeps God first.

All my children have been blessed with servants' hearts, I'm so proud of each of them. I want them to see the world, to see that they're part of God's creation and that they each have a unique role to play. I pray that Nike, Dele, Yemi, and Wale will see themselves as tools to touch humanity, and that each of them contributes to make the world a better place.

In June 2009, I took a unique group of people to Nigeria, including Sue Semrau, the head women's basketball coach at Florida State. A couple of Davidson College players who are Nigerian natives, Andrew Lovedale and

Frank Ben-Eze, made the trip with us. Sue led basketball clinics with the players, some of whom are upwards of seven feet tall, and she held her ground with these giants!

Every morning we awoke at 5:30 a.m.. We got a chance to worship God and put ourselves in His presence, and we were energized to go out and serve. Our team washed many feet, inspired many children, and I was so blessed to be able to share my story with people in my home country.

In Nigeria, there's much animosity between Muslims and Christians. It's always doubly powerful to be able to model love and show compassion to them.

We went to a leper colony to bless the people with a medical outreach, and to provide them with HIV/AIDS awareness. This colony is set aside specifically for these people, and is located so far outside the perimeter of society that they have their own system of government and their own community policing. The chief was so excited when we came to spread a message of love.

In Giro, in the northern part of the country, we went to a school where not a single one of the kids had shoes. It was like watching newborn giraffes, none of those kids had ever learned how to walk in shoes before!

One day, we went to a hospital to distribute shoes. There was a line of about 300 people when we arrived, and the first of them received their gift. And then more children showed up, hundreds and hundreds more, thousands even! There was a school about a quarter-mile from where we were, kids were dismissed for the day to come jump in line and get shoes. They were so organized, all lined up, and the line stretched out over half a mile. I wish I had a camera at that moment, it was such an incredible sight!

And, as is so often the case, we didn't have enough shoes for all of them. It was our final shoe distribution of the trip, and we just had 300 or 400 pairs left to give. Again, my heart was broken. As we left the facility, the children were running after the bus, calling out for us to please turn the bus around.

"Come back, come back," they cried.

That moment showed, once again, the immense need for what we are doing. It underscored the necessity to get the word out, recruit more helpers, bring in more volunteers, raise more financial support, and get more people to support what we're trying to accomplish. No matter how hard we work, how many shoes we give, there is always more to be done.

In Nigeria, they've never seen anything like Samaritan's Feet. People there know full well that Nigerians have something of a bad reputation in the world. They know there are people from their country who are doing things that aren't ethical, and are conducting business that does not reflect well on the motherland. But to see a Nigerian dedicate his life to giving back and helping others takes a lot of citizens and leaders in my home country by surprise. They think, "Wow, there is hope for us."

Hope is the central message I deliver everywhere I go in Nigeria. Before our shoe distributions, when I share my story at gatherings of school children, I ask, "Who wants to be a doctor? Who wants to be a pilot? Who wants to be a professor, a missionary, an attorney?"

You should see those kids, their eyes are so wide as their hands shoot straight up into the air. Hope is written across their faces. I can tell what they are thinking, "This guy is from Nigeria. My goodness! And he's doing what he's doing, following his dreams. I have dreams too, and they can be real someday!"

Each and every time, the principals and teachers came up to me afterwards and hugged me. "This is the message of hope that our kids need to hear," they'd say. "It doesn't matter what situation they find themselves in. The God of the Universe truly has a plan for them, and He can make a way where there is no way. You, Manny, are a testament to this."

We went to a part of Lagos called Ilaje, which is where the poorest of the poor live. We visited two different communities where the people live off the water, communities full of fishermen. Their children live in pure abject poverty. The school we went to had about 120 students, but this school might as well have been an abandoned shack from 100 years ago. Yet these kids were so proud of their schoolhouse. The walls were made from pieces of wood, cardboard, and whatever solid material they could find to build a four-foot high barrier against the elements. The tin roof was rusted and brown. The floor was covered in sawdust from a mill that was close by, and the teachers gave us plastic boots to wear because of all the standing water. Kids attend this school in their bare feet.

I saw this, and my soul was heavy. The hearts of our team members were broken when they saw these horrible conditions. Our dogs in the United States have better homes than this! And this was where these children went to school every day.

Then a group of people from the community came and explained the full severity of the situation to us. "These are the privileged ones," they told us. "These are the children who are able to go to school at all. This is the only schoolhouse we have, and thousands of children in our community cannot attend because it is at full capacity."

When we left Ilaje that day, I cried, "Lord, you've shown me this need, and I simply can't turn my back on this." Children in these communities need to know and believe that beyond the shoes there is hope. They need something to aspire to, something to shoot towards.

I felt the urge that we were supposed to build a school in that community. I challenged our team to do something about it. One of our team members stepped up, he was so moved that he asked to speak to the man who ran the school. "What would it take to buy this property?" he inquired. "How much would it cost to build a permanent structure for this school?"

The price for the property turned out to be $20,000, and to build the schoolhouse for 250 to 300 students would cost around $100,000. So this gentleman (who wishes to remain anonymous) told me, "Manny, I was so moved, I would love to create a challenge grant for everyone on the team to raise $1,000 to buy that property. And in addition, I want to help build this school in honor of your mother, for what she's given to this world."

When he said that, it completely tore me apart.

So we set about raising the funds to buy the property over the following nine-month period, and then we undertook the task of collecting enough money to erect the permanent structure that will bear my mother's name: Florence Ohonme.

This Christian private school is something that will stay on this earth as long as God allows us to exist on this side of heaven. It will be a safe haven where kids in that community can earn scholarships and go on to become doctors, lawyers, and community leaders.

This, to me, is the key to the future of countries like my beloved Nigeria —we must unlock the opportunities of education for kids there. If we don't invest in them, these children will be stuck in the past, caught in the endless cycle of poverty.

NUGGETS OF VIRTUE

I'm so fortunate to have been blessed with a Godly family. I have a wife who dearly loves me despite my flaws, and four children who adore me. Wherever I am, my son Wale calls me every few hours just to say, "Daddy, I love you." I didn't have anything like that growing up, and I cherish the opportunity every time I hear his voice on the phone.

And I also pray that I don't get so caught up with saving the world that I miss out on spending time with Wale and my daughters. I pray that I don't get so busy that I can't watch our children grow up. I'm becoming very cognizant of this fact, and that's why I'm trying to simplify my life. I'm searching for more people to help me on this Samaritan's Feet mission, so I can step back a little bit and invest more time with my family.

It wouldn't make sense or be God's desire if I saved 10 million children and lost the four most important ones He has given me. I've seen other ministers struggle with this dilemma. I have heard it said that one of Billy Graham's greatest regrets is that he didn't spend more time with his son, Franklin, and that was a big reason for his son's rebellion. I'm just glad that Rev. Graham's son came around to change his ways and serve God. So I'm doing everything I can to avoid going down that path.

Even though I'm the personality behind the ministry, we've always agreed that Samaritan's Feet is going to be a family ministry and we have always tried to design it as such. It's not just "Manny's stuff," it's "our stuff." I remember when we started, when our home was the warehouse. Now that we have giant warehouses all over the country, my family is still there, still helping out at every turn.

Family is one of the greatest institutions designed by God. I believe that each family is an awesome research experiment that showcases who He is. He is a great farmer, and He's not a liar. He has told us that you can never plant apple seeds and reap mango fruits. What we plant, we harvest. If we sow good seeds, we will harvest bountiful crops.

If my family didn't believe in what I do, I would not be successful. Samaritan's Feet would just be a "Manny thing." If Tracie didn't support me, this effort would have failed and folded a long time ago. My wife always tells me that the statement "behind every successful man, there is a woman" is a misnomer. It should be rewritten to say "beside" instead. And right behind that man and woman are children, whom the Lord has ordained to play key roles in His plan.

Each family is an extension of God's family, and we've all been put here with position, purpose and a place in order to accomplish His will through our lives.

Together, unified as one, God's work will be done. Amen.

12: HUMILITY

In the Nigeria of my youth, we always placed Westerners on pedestals. That's why I tell young kids in the United States today that they don't fully realize who they are as citizens, and the high value of being able to be called an American.

Some children have no idea about the doors their citizenship opens to them, the opportunity and the influence it brings. A boy from the inner city of Detroit, Chicago, or Los Angeles can go anywhere in Africa, and those kids will think he personally knew Michael Jordan! Many of these people just don't have the framework or the context to know better. All they know is that this person is an American, and they'll put he or she on a golden throne.

Now imagine that the roles are reversed. Imagine that American, or any Westerner for that matter, gets on his or her knees, on a dirt floor, looking up at those kids. We aim to serve these children of God in pure humility, speaking as the mouthpiece of the Almighty to them. They will listen to every word an American person says, from the first syllable on. They take the weight of words very seriously.

We can go and look these kids in the eyes and tell them there is hope and let them know that they are special. We can teach that there is a bright future for them because God has included them in His plan. And they believe us—they can feel it, because we are loving them! They are not sure how God's plan is going to manifest itself in their lives, but they know that it can happen. We strive to show them, through our own humility, the importance of remaining humble before the King of the Universe.

Because Coach Hunter said "Yes" and went barefoot at a basketball game, I was invited to the 2008 Final Four in San Antonio to speak at John Wooden's Legends of the Hardwood breakfast. There wasn't a dry eye in the room when I described our mission, when I told them about all those kids whose lives would be impacted by Coach Hunter's gesture.

The master of ceremonies at that breakfast was Ernie Johnson, studio host of the "Inside the NBA" show on TNT. When he shook my hand afterwards, he said, "Manny, I remember watching all of that unfold in the media and on ABC back in January. I remember telling myself that I would love to help you guys. I just didn't know why. But I'm going to talk to the producers of the show, to the president of TNT, I'm going to see if they're open to this stuff."

"Whatever you can do would be huge," I replied as I shook his hand.

I didn't know at the time that because of Ernie's Yes, God was about to swing open many big doors.

Ernie called me up a couple weeks later, and he sounded like he had just won the lottery. "Manny, Manny!" he said excitedly, "TNT wants to do something with Samaritan's Feet. You can even use our marketing staff to promote this. It's all going to happen on an amazing day."

"What day is that?" I asked in anticipation.

"Mother's Day," he exclaimed. "You know who's got a heart for children? Mothers, of course!"

He told me to come down to Atlanta on Mother's Day to be on the show and they'd have a little surprise for me. I thought maybe he would bring me on the program for two minutes or something. I didn't even have an inkling of what Ernie had in store.

When I arrived, the television guests were all in their bare feet. Kenny

Smith was there. Charles Barkley had his toenails all painted up! We had a full nine minutes to share the message of Samaritan's Feet, to tell viewers about the 300 million kids who woke up that Mother's Day morning barefoot, because their moms couldn't afford to protect their feet with shoes.

After that, things got *crazy*.

In the first four-plus years of Samaritan's Feet, we raised about 500,000 pairs of shoes. That's a significant number, but when you put that next to what we've done recently, it pales in comparison.

In 2009 alone, we raised over 1.5 million pairs of shoes. Public awareness of Samaritan's Feet went through the roof when Coach Hunter said Yes, and the amount of media coverage was mind-boggling. Donations of shoes and money poured in, enriching our ministry beyond our wildest dreams.

After the "NBA on TNT" appearance, the number of demands on my time grew. Television producers and newspaper writers wanted to specifically talk to me, as I became the face of the organization.

The sudden increase in success of Samaritan's Feet was very humbling; it was like seeing one's own baby grow from infancy to adulthood. The legs get longer, the arms get longer, and before you know it that child is walking around with its own ideas! It was amazing just to watch God in action, and all of it was of no credit to anyone but the Lord. None of us could have dreamed of what ended up happening, and nobody could have put together a marketing plan to achieve the results that God allowed us to attain.

Under the spotlight, I knew I needed to stay solidly grounded in humility. One of my favorite scriptural passages is found in Proverbs 29: "Only those who humble themselves shall be exalted." If you always stay humble, God will find the right environment and platform to lift you up in due time.

The explosion of attention didn't change my attitude or what I did on a daily basis. I still loved people like crazy, I hugged like I always hugged, and I strove to treat everybody like they're my best friends, from the doorman on the sidewalk to the CEO in the boardroom.

Nothing changed.

The only thing that was different was that we were dealing with a completely new echelon of society. Suddenly, we were talking to presidents of nations, governors, international business leaders, professional athletes, and Hollywood stars. Jack Nicholson sent a few pairs of shoes to auction off to help benefit our cause. The Philadelphia 76ers, Detroit Pistons, Memphis Grizzlies, and the Boston Celtics got involved by providing autographed basketball shoes. Calvin Brock, the boxer, has also helped us out. Many Major League Baseball players got in contact with us and asked how they could contribute.

And God showed the world that He could use a nobody from Africa to bring glory to Him. I felt like a common Joe who was empowered to fulfill a desire to bless children, operating with a vision that the divine had sent to me. It was very exciting to see people outside my regular sphere of influence be able to embrace my dream. And when all this happened, it wasn't just my vision anymore. It was the community's vision, and the world's as well.

I received calls from around the globe, letters and emails from individuals who were seeing and watching these phenomenal events unfold before their eyes. We went from an organization that was known regionally here in the southeastern United States, to a national and international organizational powerhouse with major name recognition—nearly overnight.

There was a guy named Justen who emailed me from Hong Kong. He saw the piece that ESPN did about us during our first barefoot coaching initiative and was deeply moved. He was so compelled that he wrote, "If you'll give me permission, I'm going to try and save some money. And every time there's a major event in my life, a birthday or an anniversary, I'm going to buy three pairs of shoes. Then I'm going to find three people in need living in my community. In honor to God and what He has done in you, Manny, if you'll allow me, I'm going to bless those people... in the name of the sacrifice you've made to get to where you are."

Now Justen is planning an annual music concert to benefit Samaritan's Feet in Hong Kong.

People are doing things like this by themselves, of their own volition. They feel compelled to contribute back to their own community, to help meet some of the needs there.

Because of what we've accomplished and what God has done through us, now other people are inspired to expand the cause. We have church groups, civic groups, and schools all across the world raising flip-flops and sandals, taking them to countries we're not even involved with yet. But passion has been ignited in people—they feel they can do something about this problem, and that passion is transformed into action. This is the kind of movement we want to create.

If we were to count all the shoes that have been distributed by other ministries, churches and individuals who have been inspired to do something through our vision, we'd have to add another 3 million pairs to the overall total.

In July 2008, we were able to move into a brand new facility in Fort Mill, South Carolina, right outside of Charlotte. We now have 12 full-time paid staff in our Charlotte office alone, with another 10 in Indianapolis and San Bernardino. We've tripled the number of employees in just over three years. And we can never forget our thousands of volunteers who work in our remote offices, warehouses, and mission locations around the globe.

Samaritan's Feet now operates in a 55,000 square foot office/warehouse space, serving as our worldwide central processing facility. It is also where all our corporate executives and core functional domestic and international staff work from. We also have access to 50,000 square feet of storage in Maiden, NC, and tens of thousands of available square feet in feeder warehouses around Charlotte, which we use as overflow storage.

In our local network of storage facilities, we have the ability to store as many as 500,000 pairs of shoes at any given time. Thanks to our incredible recent growth, we now have three major warehouses across the United States. In addition to our central North Carolina hub, we have a storage facility in San Bernardino, California and another in Indianapolis, Indiana. Our Indianapolis facility is our biggest one, we can store over 600,000 pairs of shoes there. On any given day, there are hundreds of local volunteers who are in that warehouse, processing shoes.

We experienced phenomenal growth, in spite of what I would call a general famine in the financial world. I tell people we operate in God's economy, which doesn't fluctuate when Wall Street goes up or down. God's economy doesn't go crazy when the pundits on CNN or CNBC report bad news. We are not defined by those indicators, and we've been very truly fortunate as a result.

I've always been a believer that God would get things to you if He can get them *through* you. We've been a conduit of that blessing. He's entrusted millions of dollars' worth of footwear to Samaritan's Feet to use as instruments of mercy and love. We are so honored that we can be a vehicle to bless people in the world.

Coach Hunter's "Yes" touched off chain reactions everywhere. After all the media coverage, one of the major shoe manufacturers said that they couldn't do business with us anymore. It was a corporate decision, they informed us, and it came about because some in their organization felt we were positioning ourselves as too overtly faith-based. They wanted to remain staunchly religion-neutral. For whatever reason, they let us know that they wouldn't donate any more of their shoes for our distributions.

We were devastated.

Shortly thereafter, some folks at the U.S. Department of Homeland Security in California saw one of the CNN pieces about us. A high-ranking official there was so inspired and moved by what we were doing, she contacted us.

"Are you guys for real?" the woman asked me. She couldn't believe the scope of what we were doing.

She told me that Homeland Security confiscates over one million pairs of counterfeit shoes every year in California alone, shoes that by law are not allowed to enter the United States. The owners of these brands the counterfeiters copy are protected by trade and tariff regulations, so Homeland Security is under strict obligation to intercept the shoes before they can reach the American market. But when that woman saw what we did, she knew she had to go to bat for us.

It doesn't matter to a child walking on broken glass and rocks where a pair of shoes came from—all that matters is that those shoes protect their feet. This woman went to the shoe companies, contacted executives, went up the chain of command at these corporations as high as she could go. "We've found a conduit that could be a huge beneficiary of these shoes," she would tell them. "Samaritan's Feet is touching people, and inspiring kids around the world."

Homeland Security first donated 10,000 pairs of shoes to us in 2008 as part of Coach Hunter's first barefoot coaching campaign, and we shipped them to Mozambique and Swaziland. Shortly thereafter, the man who had called us before to tell us that his company couldn't do business with us anymore called me back.

"Manny," he said. "Do you think you could handle 253,000 pairs of our shoes?"

We couldn't believe it. If you think about the street value of 253,000 pairs of shoes, that's more than $12 million!

This just shows how big God is, and how far He will go to accomplish His mission. If He can use a donkey to communicate (Numbers 22), for crying out loud, what else can God use?! Since then, this major shoe company has been a huge partner of ours.

One of the most incredible end-results of Coach Hunter's "Yes" came about when Kmart donated one million pairs of shoes to Samaritan's Feet after Ernie Johnson's "Yes" on TNT. Another was our encounter with Indiana governor Mitch Daniels, who said "Yes" and used his own platform as a way to help needy children.

We approached Governor Daniels because we were looking for a warehouse to store this million pairs of shoes. One of our big supporters is the head of one of the major logistics providers in that state, and he had a connection to the governor's office. He heard that the state was only using 10 percent of the storage capacity of state warehouses for which Indiana had already paid long-term leases. We already have an office in Indianapolis, where Todd Melloh and his marketing operations are located. Once I heard the news about the empty warehouses, I knew we had to act.

Here was our idea: if the state was willing to donate 75,000 square feet of storage to Samaritan's Feet for the storage of 700,000 pairs of shoes, we would use the state's prison inmates to sort and process them. It would give the inmates a purpose and a mission that was bigger than themselves, to allow them to be involved in something positive.

"Everywhere I go across this state, people are talking about IUPUI and what Ron did," Governor Daniels told me. "I know all the good that you guys are doing."

He agreed to champion our cause. But then I had another idea.

We had coaches going barefoot, why not a barefoot politician?

Governor Daniels is known as a non-traditional and unconventional leader in his home state of Indiana, and he was excited at the chance to be the first barefoot governor in the history of the United States.

"I'll do it!" he exclaimed when we brought up the idea. We didn't have to ask him twice!

On Friday, January 16, 2009, Governor Daniels held a press conference in his bare feet. All the local media were there, as were Coach Hunter and myself. The entire staff at the statehouse went barefoot, some of the state senators did too.

"I'm challenging all of Indiana to get behind this," the governor announced at the press conference. "There are 300 million children in the world without shoes. We all have a platform, and I choose to use mine to be a voice for those kids."

The Associated Press wrote a story about the event, which was reprinted in newspapers all across the world.

Before I left that day, Governor Daniels asked me, "Is there anything else I can do? Please let me know. I want to help more."

I asked him if he could connect us with other governors. "Sure," he said. Personally, I thought we were just making polite small-talk.

But by two o'clock that afternoon, Governor Daniels' office was back in touch with us. The governors of Hawaii, Wisconsin, South Dakota, Illinois and West Virginia had expressed support, and wanted to help the cause. Within 24 hours, they all had their own barefoot events planned. From Arkansas to Oklahoma, there was this barefoot ripple effect throughout the nation's state houses.

Later in the spring, at a function in Charlotte, I was introduced to Andre Bauer, the lieutenant governor of South Carolina. He told me, "After I heard about what happened that January day at the Indiana state house, I knew I had to meet with you." We exchanged cards and agreed to get in touch after I returned from our summer mission trips.

When I got back, he called me up, and I shared some of the things our teams had seen overseas. He was so moved by my stories. "I want to do something similar to what Governor Daniels did," he said. "But I want to try doing something even *bigger*. What can South Carolina do for you?"

"No, no," I said. "The real question is, 'What can *we* do for the poor kids in South Carolina?'"

"I'd like to invite you to a special assembly of our state senate," Lt. Gov. Bauer said. "I'd be honored if you'd be my guest."

Everything happened so fast! A few hours later, I was at the state capitol in Columbia.

I met Lt. Gov. Bauer in a back chamber, he put on an official gown and we walked together towards the senate floor, accompanied by his entourage. We got to the front of the senate hall, and the doors swung open.

"Here comes the lieutenant governor, president of the senate, Andre Bauer," a voice boomed.

Everybody stood up. He swept to the front, banged the gavel, called the session to order. Everyone sat back down, and the doors shut behind us.

"And now, the guest of the lieutenant governor, Emmanuel 'Manny' Ohonme from Charlotte, North Carolina," the voice boomed again.

I entered the floor of the state senate, and everybody stood up. The entire assembly gave me a long standing ovation, it sounded like thunder in there.

You would have thought I was the visiting King of Nigeria or something!

As I was walking down that aisle with all those people standing and applauding, I thought about history. Here I was, an African-American in a state that had such a painful racially-charged past, and I was being treated with so much honor. I thought about how this state house once flew a confederate battle flag from the top as recently as the year 2000. To see the love and the respect they showed an African boy from Lagos was overwhelming. They escorted me to my seat, and I watched as they debated some legislation.

After about 15 minutes, Lt. Gov. Bauer stood up. He started talking about Samaritan's Feet and what we were doing in the world. I couldn't believe the research he had done. He was listing all these countries we had been to, and even recited my biography. One by one, the senators stood up and came over to where I was sitting. Each one of them shook my hand.

I was floating two feet off that floor; I felt like I was dreaming!

Afterwards, I met with many of the state senators and they asked me the same question that Lt. Gov. Bauer had posed. "Manny, what can South Carolina do for you?"

"In my heart, I know there are so many thousands of kids in this state who can't afford shoes for their feet," I answered. "I want to see if we can collaborate, and organize a statewide back-to-school initiative this summer to get those kids some new shoes."

A few weeks later, we had a meeting of South Carolina political leaders, civic leaders, and pastors from some of the biggest churches across the state. The chairman and president of the state United Way attended as well. I took the floor and presented my vision: to impact 50,000 South Carolina kids at multiple locations in all 40 counties across the state. Everybody was behind it.

"I only have one condition I'd like to present," I said. "Our partners who are going to help us be the channel for distribution in the poor communities have to be the churches. That's how we do this."

The politicians were immediately skeptical, believing that we couldn't do anything like that, citing the separation of church and state. By law, there's not to be any collaboration between government and religious institutions.

"But this has nothing to do with labels and divisions," I explained. "We need pastors in poor communities, the governor's office, the United Way, the department of education, social services all working together to help these poor kids. The church is the institution that's going to be in that community when Samaritan's Feet is gone. That's who is going to follow up with these kids. The churches are going to be building long-term relationships with those families."

Everybody finally agreed. On June 13 we tried a pilot program where we reached over 400 kids in four different locations around one of the state's counties. To promote the event, Lt. Gov. Bauer went barefoot on the floor of the South Carolina state senate. During the distribution, we all meshed as one: charities, churches, community leaders, as well as politicians at the state and local level. It was so amazing to see; one team united for a common cause. And we washed those kids' feet and gave them new socks and shoes. For a few minutes, we made each of those poor children feel like they were the richest people in the world.

As of this writing, we've performed over 50 projects all across South Carolina and impacted over 15,000 children towards our goal of 50,000. We now have a proven model of wide-scale collaboration involving a diverse group of institutions, working together to get things done for a greater good.

God has many ways of keeping His servants humble.

In spite of all the success that Samaritan's Feet enjoyed after our national breakthrough, there were doubts as to our very survival as a ministry. At the beginning of December, 2008, it was the first time in many years that we got close to the edge. As 2008 ended, I really wondered if we would be around to see 2009.

We had beaten the odds, and thrived in a year during which many charities were forced to shut their doors due to America's drastic economic downturn. And we had the biggest opportunity in our history on the horizon: the one million pairs of shoes that had been donated to us by Kmart. We were going to do our second annual barefoot coaching campaign in January. The number of initiatives we had going on all over the world was rapidly increasing.

But we only had about $10,000 in the bank. Before I had gone on our World Walk in October, some key sponsors that had pledged to come through financially found themselves hit hard by the general economic collapse in the United States. They had to withdraw their support. One of them was a huge developer in North Carolina who was hurt badly when the housing market plummeted.

So we had to assume many of the costs related to the World Walk, plus logistics expenses for unexpected donations of thousands of shoes, which severely depleted our resources.

"How in the world are we going to make our December payroll?" I wondered aloud. "How are we going to pay to ship all these containers of shoes that are going around the world?"

Sears told us that we had only two weeks to move the shoes they had donated. I was very concerned that Samaritan's Feet had become so big that it was about to collapse.

This weighed on me like crazy. I always try so hard to be 100 percent positive and have bottomless energy all the time, but it was taking all the effort I had to make it through a day. Not many knew what was going on, just a few people in my inner circle. While I tried to maintain a positive outlook during the day, I suffered through sleepless nights, tossing and turning, wondering what was going to happen.

Every morning at 3 a.m., I was awake. I prayed and prayed. Tracie would wake up and ask me, "What's going on?"

"Honey, I don't know how we're going to make it," I said. "We have $10,000. Our bills for this month are $171,000. I don't know what to do!"

It was one thing to look for a few thousand here or there, and ask for a miracle from God. But $171,000! In ten days! I didn't know if there were any miracles that big. Or that fast! We only had *ten days* to make it happen!

We were faced with an economy in which people weren't giving, with companies going under left and right. But Samaritan's Feet had a staff that needed to be paid. Our staff loves us, and each of them loves the children we help enough to do it for free, but they also have families and responsibilities. We had financial obligations too—the trucking companies that transport our shoes don't do business with us based on my good looks alone! They want to get paid, brother!

On the first Friday of December 2008, I was ready to throw in the towel. "Where are you, God?" I prayed. "I've done what You told me to do, I'm out there doing all this stuff. You've given us all these blessings this year. So now You're going to let us *burn* like this?"

There was no way we could have come up with $171,000. I was convinced of it. Where was all that money going to come from? I made a round of phone calls, trying to raise the funds from every well-heeled person I knew. Nothing.

Everybody was in survival mode, afraid that every cent they donated would put them one penny closer to the poorhouse.

"God, I'm desperate," I prayed that Saturday night (at 3 a.m. again). "Next week is payroll and all our bills are due. I'm struggling, I need You so much right now. I just need to know where this is going to come from. Give me a clue. Please, God."

I went to church with my family that Sunday. We sang, we prayed. I don't think I've ever prayed so hard in my life. After praise and worship, the choir director stood up and announced, "If anybody needs prayer, please come up to the front."

I didn't budge. This was between me and God, I thought to myself. God and I had already had this conversation every night for a week. He'd heard my plea over and over! I had done everything I could. His reputation was on the line now. It had nothing to do with me. At least that's what I was thinking.

But then I felt this conviction in my spirit. "You are being prideful," I told myself. "You need to get up there and be prayed for. Move! Go!"

So I stuck my tail between my legs and walked to the front of that church before that congregation. One of the board members, a good friend of mine, was up there. He asked me, "What do you want me to pray with you about, Manny?"

I told him, "Tom, I need you to pray for a miracle. I've seen God perform a lot of miracles, but this is the first time I've ever been really nervous. I can't give you the details, because this is between me and God. But I'm telling you, brother, I need a miracle to happen in the next few days."

We prayed, and then Tom hugged me and I returned to my seat. Normally, I'm the ultimate optimist. I'm Mr. Hope all the time. Another of my good friends, Louie, saw my face that day in church and quickly realized something was wrong. The hope was diminishing from my eyes.

After the end of the service, Louie cornered me in the back of the church. "Manny, what's going on?" he asked me.

"I'm fine, man," I replied. I was putting up the best front I could.

Louie was persistent. "No, seriously, what's going on?"

"I'm praying for a miracle," I said.

Louie told me that he would fast at breakfast every morning for the next seven days, and pray for me during those times. "But you've got to commit to one thing for me, Manny," he told me. "When God grants you that miracle, you have to give me a call and let me know."

I was touched, but I was still so down that I wasn't able to be fully convinced. "Sure thing, buddy," I said. We hugged and high-fived, and we went on our way.

One of our supporters had told me the previous Friday that he wanted me to come see him. He asked if I would speak to the staff at his supply-chain logistics company. At the time, it was just another item on my to-do list. On Monday morning, I checked the calendar and went over to one of his offices along with Ron Pegram, Samaritan's Feet's chief operating officer.

We were there to give a talk, to challenge the staff to take on Samaritan's Feet as their company's official charitable campaign. Employees could choose to have a certain amount of money—$10, $50 or $100—taken out of their paychecks every month as a donation instead of directly writing us a check. This is the kind of campaign that the United Way often uses.

I thought I was going down to see him for this meeting. But as I often say, our future is God's history. I didn't know God's hands were at work that day, and that He had spoken to another man about my plight. Before our talk, the executive who was championing our cause with the company (who wishes to remain anonymous) brought us into his office and had us sit down.

"How are things going with Samaritan's Feet?" he asked.

"Everything's going very well," I said with as straight a face as I could manage. "I have to raise a couple hundred thousand dollars in the next week. But other than that, everything's good."

He smiled, and continued with his line of questioning. "How's the orphan feeding program you've been working on? How's that going?"

"That's going really well," I replied. "Despite the fact that we have to raise $171,000 very soon or we'll go belly up, the orphan feeding program is going great."

This got him laughing. "Wow, you're in this dichotomy, Manny," he exclaimed. "Everything's going great except for the fact you're broke."

"Yeah," I confessed. "You've got the idea of exactly where we are."
Then he said something that startled me. "Manny, you won't believe this.
This weekend, I felt a conviction that I'm supposed to help you."

"Here's something I want to do for you," he continued. "I want to
challenge you. I'm going to give you two $100,000 matching grants. But
here's the caveat: you have 10 days to go raise the money. If you raise
$100,000 in 10 days, I'll match it with $100,000. If you raise another
$100,000 in the same timeframe, I'll match that too. One grant is for shoes,
and the other is for the orphans."

I couldn't believe his offer. I looked over at Ron, and he couldn't
believe it either.

"I don't know if I should jump or scream," I said. "Nobody's giving in
these tough economic times. You've given me one of those unattainable,
impossible tasks... you're telling me I have to raise $100,000 to get
$100,000? I can't even raise $1,000 these days!"

"Manny," he replied, smiling. "How you get it done is between you and
God."

It was a good day. Later in the conference room, the company's leaders
decided to support us by starting a Samaritan's Feet Giving Campaign,
deducting donations from paychecks. Right before I left, my friend the
executive cut me a check for $42,000. "I'm fronting you this," he said.
"Because I trust that you'll be able to raise the rest."

And then, when we returned to Charlotte, it was time to get down to
the business of raising six figures in ten days. This was a major undertaking,
and it was time to trust God.

But lo and behold, within seven days, we had raised $142,000. In just
seven days. Nobody was giving anything previously, but that week the
floodgates opened wide.

I don't know why people just started giving in a time when the economy
was completely upside down. If I had that answer, I'd apply to be God's
special assistant, His top messenger! Individuals who didn't give before,
who had refused or declined our previous approaches, were suddenly
giving. And they were digging deep, too: $5,000 and $10,000 donations. I
was blown away by all of this.

It wasn't as if we had built a new website or started a fresh, exciting initiative. The matching grants simply gave me a different way of asking people than I had before, and this made all the difference. "In the next ten days, every dollar you give Samaritan's Feet will be doubled," I was able to tell people. "I have someone willing to write a check for $100,000 if I raise that same amount. Would you help me reach this goal?"

I remember receiving that matching-grant check for $100,000, and I was just beside myself.

"Look what God did," I said aloud as I stared at all those zeroes on that check. "*Look what God did!*"

We came short of the amount necessary for the second matching grant, but we raised our payroll and settled all of Samaritan's Feet's bills for the month. But even though we didn't raise the full amount, we got a chance to raise money we wouldn't have raised if we hadn't gone through this process.

I remember calling my buddy Louie a few days later. "God came through," I exclaimed. "He granted that miracle!"

"That was just another test to remind you," Louie replied. "As long as you're in this, Manny, God has your back. You should never forget that. He just wants you to make sure you stay obedient."

In the midst of our greatest successes, at the end of an incredible year, God found a way to reinforce my humility. He just wanted me to abandon my pride, and He reminded me who was really in charge.

Tracie often reminds me that God wants us to always be 100 percent dependent on Him. She once told me, "Manny, work as hard as you can, as if everything depends on you. But pray as hard as you can, as if everything depends on God. Do both of those things, and you will have success that no man can ever explain."

This simple recipe is a fantastic blueprint for success. I know it has been in my life.

NUGGETS OF VIRTUE

I have never wanted to draw attention to myself. One of my biggest challenges is to avoid getting in the way of what God is doing. It's not about me; it has everything to do with Him. I never want to put myself on a pedestal, and I don't want to imply, "Look at me and what I've accomplished."

My policy is to allow the fruits of God's actions to do the speaking. Matthew 7:16 tells us, "By their fruits you shall recognize them." I've always believed that.

But it's come to the point that people, all my friends and advisors, have told me that I have to step forward.

"This is a story of hope," somebody told me recently. "This is not just your journey. This is a story of family, friends, and partners. It is an account that will inspire many others to action. And it will show people that whatever they are going through, there is always hope."

I never want to receive glory for something that God has done. I believe that I'm a link God is using to bring hope to the hopeless, a voice to allow the voiceless to speak out loud. I was recently talking with a gentleman who attends a church where I spoke and he said, "Manny, when you were at our church, God was revealing this picture to me. He is truly using you to raise an army of children who will all rise above the despair and poverty and pursue their dreams. You are a hope ambassador to the world."

I believe that out of those millions of people we've touched through Samaritan's Feet, there's another Manny out there. Maybe he's in Nigeria, Peru, Guyana, or living in any of these impoverished countries that we've been fortunate enough to bless. There have to be a lot of Mannys who the Lord has strategically hand-picked to influence and change this world. But we have to go and show them God's love so we can keep the dream alive in their hearts. We have to keep reminding them of that dream, and keep inspiring them to reach higher.

Everywhere I go, I have the opportunity to talk to hundreds and thousands of children, and share the story of what God has done in my life. I tell them about hope, not just the hope of African boys like me, but the hope of girls and boys all over the world. The thing that excites me is that I have the opportunity to stand in front of them and look into their eyes. It's like magnets between my eyes and theirs; we click, and they're focused and dialed in. And when I have their complete and undivided attention, I want to let them know that God can do amazing things through their lives. Just as long as they are willing to surrender, be obedient, be faithful, and say Yes.

If I can come out of a cinder-block house in Lagos, Nigeria, and accomplish all that God has done through me, then I know for a fact that the same big dream is available to children everywhere. My message to kids is that there is such a thing as "big" in terms of dreaming, and that "bigness" is available to all of God's children.

"Wow, Manny is one of us," I hope they're saying to themselves. "He once had no shoes, and now he's providing food and shoes to millions of people worldwide. And he's talking to me, telling me to chase my dream!"

That's what I consider real hope. I don't know who's sitting in that audience, where they are in their walk, or what their struggles and challenges are. But I do know that all it takes is God bringing somebody to say the right thing at the right time. I try to be a passionate inspiration, to remind people that God can help them soar above all obstacles. Their goals might seem as far away as the moon today, but the God of the Universe has already strategically ordered their steps so they can achieve their dreams tomorrow.

I can't wait to hear their stories!

WHAT'S YOUR SOLE PURPOSE?

Obedience is one of the hardest things to submit to. However, it's the greatest gift we can give to God. It is a trait that is prevalent in a life filled with purpose.

We were all brought to earth for a reason, and God wants to reveal it to us. He does this through prayer, our experiences, and other people speaking into our lives. Unfortunately, many times we go our own way, get ahead of Him, or just simply say no to what He is calling us to do. We always need to remember we are here to bring glory to God. We honor Him through our obedience. Coach Hunter did, and so have many others before him as well.

Our legacy should be created based on what we do for others, not on how much money we make or how many material things we acquire. We will never know the impact of the ripple effect of our actions and obedience if we sit on the sidelines as spectators.

Can you imagine facing God one day and He says, "I had so much more in store for you, but you rarely ever listened to Me or said 'Yes' to what I asked you to do."

We would be devastated. The Lord knows every gift He gave us and every desire in our heart, but many times we fail to act or use them to glorify Him.

It's very similar to a young man who has the ability to play sports at a high level because he was given athletic abilities by the Creator. However, he refuses to work hard at improving his skills and tries to get by based on his natural abilities, rather than outworking everyone. He takes the path of least resistance and fails to live up to the plan God had for him when He blessed him with these natural abilities.

Remember, the effort is ours, but the results belong to God. Therefore, some people fail to reach the full potential that those around them recognize they have. As a result, they fail at something that the Lord gave them naturally because others outworked them, or because they were not obedient to what God called them to do. The platform that might have been used and the success that would have come never materializes—all because God-given gifts are wasted.

What natural abilities and gifts has your heavenly Father given you? What comes easy for you? How can you use these talents to reach others for the Kingdom? Maybe it's fundraising, marketing, logistics, accounting, or legal skills. Are you a Sunday school teacher at your church? Or are you gifted as a graphic artist or a web designer? Do you know some people with the financial means to help others? Maybe your family has been financially secure for quite some time and you are looking for "Kingdom Impact."

Samaritan's Feet needs people like you, and more importantly, so does God.

He is searching for men and women who will say YES and use their platform and skill-sets to reach more children like Manny. Can you imagine the stories that you could share with others if you were able to reach one child, who then paid it forward to reach 10 million people in over 50 countries?

Do you think that Dave knew that the little boy he touched, would impact millions of other people worldwide demonstrating God's love? There's no way Dave could have ever imagined such an outcome. Only God can do something so miraculous and marvelous.

What ripples do you want to create?

As you were reading this book, perhaps you were wondering, "What is God asking me to say 'Yes' to? What gifts has He given me that I am using or not using? What platform do I have to make a difference? How can I provide a voice for the voiceless? How can one person possibly make a difference? How many more Mannys are out there that I could help reach? Could I meet a little girl and affect her the same way that Dave did Manny?"

The answer is yes to most of your questions, but the obedience factor is absolutely necessary. Whatever your job, wherever you are financially, whatever your age, you can make a tremendous difference. God is looking high and low for people like you to be obedient.

Samaritan's Feet is praying that more people like you will say Yes.

What is God asking you to do for Samaritan's Feet? What part will you play? There are countless ways to help. You can assist with shipping expenses, provide legal support, conduct a shoe drive at your church or school, help update our website, join the barefoot movement by creating your own event, create your own idea, become an area coordinator to lead your team in your community, hold a fundraiser. You can invite Manny to speak to your school, church, business, civic group, or lead a mission team. You can volunteer at the warehouse, or go on a shoe distribution trip.

You can support Samaritan's Feet by conducting a "Shoes of Hope" drive in your community. We need $5 per pair of shoes to help us defray the costs of shipping and delivering each pair of shoes to the needy!

You can help us raise money, donate money, become a voice for the voiceless, work in one of our regional offices as a volunteer, share this story to others or write to us and find out what our needs are.

Or you can pass this book on to someone else to read, even purchase a few copies to present as gifts to others!

Again, what is your sole purpose?

So many of us believe that we have no worthy gift to offer humanity. Many are of the opinion the world is too big to change. One of the greatest excuses I hear is "I'm a nobody," a phrase that inhibits us from making a difference in the world.

It's a lie.

Each of us is created in the image of God. His Word promises us abilities and power big enough to change the world. You are included in God's will, as long as you have breath and oxygen flowing through your lungs.

Your purpose for existence is to love God and His creation, and your life and legacy will be to make Him known to others. Remember the words of Luke 12:48: "From everyone who has been given much, much will be demanded; and from the one who has been entrusted with much, much more will be asked."

Your greatest contribution to humanity is your response to the Lord's call, and your blessings will flow relative to the measure of your obedience. God has instilled in you a capacity for action. He has empowered you to illuminate social issues, to galvanize change, and to pay it forward. He has given you the strength to motivate and inspire, and the courage to show others how to make the most of their own lives.

Too often, we allow comfort and complacency to distract us from our divine assignment. Don't start tomorrow; you are only guaranteed today. Procrastination is a thief of time. If you wait to begin living out your sole purpose, the shameful regrets of an unfulfilled destiny will fill your days. Tomorrow will become a week of tomorrows, and months will turn into years.

Don't be robbed of your destiny. You were created for greatness. You were born to make a difference and *change your world*.

What ripples do you plan to make? What work will outlive you and create an everlasting impact, effects that will only be revealed when your time on earth is complete?

Say "Yes" to whatever God is asking you to do for Him today. It will change your life, guaranteed. It changed mine. Believe!

ACKNOWLEDGMENTS

EMMANUEL "MANNY" OHONME

To two of my most notable friends in the world, Colin Pinkney and David Fincher, and their beloved brides Terri and Amy, respectively. You were pillars of encouragement and strength to Tracie and me. Thank you for believing in the vision early on, when no one else believed. Thank you Frank and Christine Cantadore, for inspiring me and telling me to pour myself into whatever the Lord chooses to bless the most in my life. The product of this advice has been the success of Samaritan's Feet. Thank you! To Harry and Lydia Sangree, for investing and challenging me to write this book. To all my board members and advisors (past and present): Raj and Meena Pragasam, Paul and Wanda Thompson, Wes and Toni Cruickshank, Doug and Rebecca Stafford, Rev. Mike and Sharon Stevens, Scott and Rebecca Carr, Mark and Marlene Moosa, Kris and Larry Meyers, Grant and Lisa Wilson, Hal and Angie Hawisher, Toby and Alisa Tate, Peter and Tanya Rieke, Matthew and Jolly Kuruvilla, Linda and Rick Cherry, Michael and Lynné Crowder, Bill and Luanne Parmelee, Jim and Anne Hoefflin, Dr. Kehinde and Femi Tokunboh, Wacyf and Nadia Ghali, Jonathan and Vivienne Ramsey, Phillip and Gladys Nelson, Kwesi Kamau, Herb Johnson, Leroy Matthews, Perry Tuttle, Marcus Smith, Phil Cohn, Eric Lewis, J Rollins, Keith White, Cathy Hendricks, and Bob Emory. To my pastors

Mike and Denise Fields and Rex and Chris Bornman, who have fed me spiritually for years and remind me to continue pursuing the Christ Life with humility.

To the wonderful staff and volunteers of Samaritan's Feet who work tirelessly daily in America and around the world through our "Shoes of Hope"" relief missions. You are bringing a life-changing message of hope, peace, and love to destitute children in need with dignity and compassion. Thank you.

To Paul Thompson, Toby Tate, and the Transportation Insight families, thank you for making yourselves an extension of this vision and allowing your hearts to beat for the children of the world.

To all our wonderful supporters and partners, we are here and thriving today because of your love for children and your generosity. Only eternity will reveal the impact we've been able to make together, because you said "Yes" to support the vision of Samaritan's Feet.

To everyone who has donated shoes, prayed, supported us financially, gone on a mission domestically or internationally, or worked in the warehouse to sort and process shoes, in support of this ministry. Thank you.

To Kyle Whelliston for saying "Yes" to help me write this book. I have seen a transformation in you throughout this process. Thank you for your obedience and sacrifice to the Lord.

To Michael Crowder and the team at Barefoot Legacies & Publishing: our best days are still ahead. Thanks for believing so much in this project and for seeing it through!

To Mike and Becky Pitman, thanks for responding to the Lord's unction after watching my interview on Inside the NBA on TNT. Your contribution to this ministry will never be forgotten. You've been a rock and a great sounding board for me. May the Lord continue to inspire you to say "Yes" to His calling!

To Todd Melloh and his beloved wife Carrie, I thank the Lord for you daily and for saying the ultimate "Yes" to join Samaritan's Feet. Your obedience to the Lord and perseverance has helped to create one of the greatest ministries I have ever known. Your God-given creativity has helped to take the ministry of Samaritan's Feet to another level. Thank you.

To Coach Hunter of IUPUI (our first barefoot coach), Sue Semrau of Florida State (our first female coach), Ernie Johnson, Charles Barkley, Kenny Smith of Inside the NBA on TNT, Governor Mitch Daniels of Indiana (our first barefoot Governor) and other Governors and Lt. Governors of states and the hundreds of college, pros, high school, middle school and recreational league coaches around the world that have coached barefoot or shed their shoes on behalf of the over 300 million children on our planet who would never be able to afford a pair of shoes. Thank you for using your platform and position to be the voice for these children. Your sacrifice has blessed millions of children in America and people in need in over 50 countries around the world. Thank you!

To Kmart for donating our first 1 million pairs of shoes and to Crocs, Converse, Fila, Homeland Security, Renaissance Imports and the hundreds of corporations that have contributed to the plight of shoeless orphans and vulnerable children in this country and overseas. Thank you!

To Damien Horne for putting lyrics to the mission of Samaritan's Feet. Thanks for writing our song and reminding me of the importance of Dreaming. I'll never forget you and our friends who joined me for two weeks on our 300-mile World Walk journey from Charlotte to Atlanta, on behalf of the 300 million children we serve. Thank you for taking the hill!

To Tom and Karrie Wilkens, my in laws John and Victoria Hanson, and all our friends who have sacrificed and watched our most precious assets (our children) whenever we can't take them with us on the mission field. Tracie and I are forever grateful to you!

To my bride Tracie and our four children, thanks for loaning me to the world to serve my King! I thank you for all you do in support of the mission of Samaritan's Feet. Your sacrifice will never be forgotten and will one day be rewarded.

To my Lord and Savior Jesus Christ, for saving me and granting me Grace and the opportunity to say "Yes" to follow Him.

KYLE WHELLISTON

Special thanks to my dear friend Roni Lagin for designing this book. Thanks also to Damon Mosley for the deadline inspiration.

I'd like to thank Douglas Fairchild, Irene Justinski, Bill and Murray for their valuable contributions. Thanks to Ron Hunter, Todd Melloh, Bruce Bodman, and all the staff at Samaritan's Feet for their kind help. Thanks also to my former editors at ESPN for allowing me to write the article that led to this project, and to all my friends in The Mid-Majority for their love and support over the past five years.

A world–no, a universe of thanks to the entire Ohonme family for their graciousness, cooperation, patience and understanding during the production of this book. Manny, my brother, I'll always appreciate this blessed opportunity.

This book is based on interviews that took place in Lima, Peru in July 2009, during a Samaritan's Feet mission trip. My most heartfelt thanks to master translator Oscar Malca, Yemina Santa Maria, and Pastor Samuel Santa Maria. I'd like to recognize my SF teammates Lori Frazier Shrum, Steve Kinney, Jeff Lamb, and Zach Schuman, whose support and friendship that week I will always remember.

I dedicate my efforts on this project to all the children of Lurin and Pachahutec, and to Soledad most of all. Dios te bendiga.

A SPECIAL REQUEST

To help us reach our goal of putting 10 million pairs of shoes on the feet of 10 million impoverished children in the next 10 years, or to order more copies of this book, please visit us on the Web at:

www.samaritansfeet.org

www.mannyohonme.com

wwwSoulPurposeBook.com

I would love to hear your thoughts about Sole Purpose and our mission. You can email me at manny@samaritansfeet.org.

It costs Samaritan's Feet $5 to help process, ship, and deliver a pair of shoes. You can text a donation of $5 to help change a life by texting our keyword SHOES to 85944 and $5 will be added to your phone bill. You can do this up to five times per month—that will be five children you can impact every month.

Thanks in advance for your support.

"My life, all that I have, all that I am, and all that I have been given, is too valuable to simply be hoarded for my own temporary purposes. I choose to invest. I choose to give. I choose to serve. I choose to make a difference. I choose to leave a lasting legacy.

— Manny Ohonme, Founder and President, Samaritan's Feet.

TO LEARN MORE ABOUT SAMARITAN'S FEET
OR TO SCHEDULE THE AUTHOR FOR SPEAKING
ENGAGEMENTS OR SPECIAL EVENTS, CONTACT:

EMMANUEL OHONME
FOUNDER AND PRESIDENT
SAMARITAN'S FEET INTERNATIONAL
P.O. BOX 78992
CHARLOTTE, NC 28271

PHONE: 704-341-1630
TOLL FREE: 866-833-SHOE

EMAIL: manny@samaritansfeet.org
INTERNET: www.samaritansfeet.org
www.mannyohonnme.com

To view a short video presentation about
Samaritan's Feet, visit www.samaritansfeet.org

Join our Facebook Communities:
Shoes of Hope Ambassadors (Official Site),
or Barefoot for a Cause.

One of the best ways you can help support
Samaritan's Feet is to order a quantity of Sole Purpose
books to place in the hands of individuals, churches, or
corporations. We need an army of people who will catch
the vision. You can place your order either by phoning
888-777-1896 or at www.SolePurposeBook.com.

SAMARITAN'S FEET
servant hearts ... sharing hope

Text SHOES to 85944

866-833-SHOE (7463) • www.samaritansfeet.org